# Reading for Redemption

# Reading for Redemption

*Practical Christian Criticism*

CHRISTIAN R. DAVIS

WIPF & STOCK · Eugene, Oregon

READING FOR REDEMPTION
Practical Christian Criticism

"Constantly Risking Absurdity (#15)" By Lawrence Ferlinghetti, from
A CONEY ISLAND OF THE MIND, copyright ©1958 by Lawrence
Ferlinghetti. Reprinted by permission of New Directions Publishing Corp.

"The Red Wheelbarrow" By William Carlos Williams, from THE
COLLECTED POEMS: VOLUME I, 1909–1939, copyright ©1938 by New
Directions Publishing Corp. Reprinted by permission of New Directions
Publishing Corp.

Scriptures are taken from the NEW KING JAMES VERSION. Copyright ©
1979, 1980, 1982, Thomas Nelson, Inc., Publishers.

Wipf & Stock
An Imprint of Wipf and Stock Publishers
199 W. 8th Ave., Suite 3
Eugene, OR 97401

www.wipfandstock.com

ISBN 13: 978-1-61097-064-8

Manufactured in the U.S.A.

#708091117

# Contents

# 1

## Redemption: The Foundation of Literature

IN THIS book, I make two major claims: first, that the pattern of creation, fall, and redemption is the foundation for all literature; and second, that the ways in which literature affects readers are determined by the ways in which that literature portrays redemption. These claims may be unpopular for at least two reasons. One is that my first claim goes against the prevailing trends of postmodernism by making an assertion about "the foundation for all literature." Such a generalization will sound simplistic at best, yet I believe that I have provided a great deal of concrete evidence to support it. The second is that my claims are based on assumptions that connect to Christianity. I have even called this theory "Christian criticism," although I hesitate to do so. Its underlying assumptions do come out of Christianity. However, they are assumptions that anyone can consider, regardless of differing religious or philosophical positions. Its methodology does not imply any particular religious belief. And it works equally well for all types of literature and all types of readers. Nevertheless, I have called this theory Christian criticism because, as I said, its underlying assumptions do come from Christianity, and therefore it will be Christian readers, first of all, who may be most sympathetic to my proposals. Furthermore, those who already believe that Christianity is the universal explanation of reality—who believe that Jesus is "the way, the truth, and the life" —are most likely to accept the explanatory power of this theory.

To put it another way, if Christians believe that their way of seeing the world is the correct way, then their way of interpreting literature should be the correct way. Various current literary theories claim to link literature to what "really" matters. At the risk of oversimplifying, one could say that each theory is defined by its claim of what is most significant in life. If the Marxists have it right, then the economic struggle over the means of production is what finally matters. If the feminists are right, then gender is at the heart of everything. To postmodern theorists, power and human conflict are the ground of everything. As Terry Eagleton says in *Literary Theory: An Introduction*:

> The feminist critic is not studying representations of gender simply because she believes that this will further her political ends. She also believes that gender and sexuality are central themes in literature and other sorts of discourse, and that any critical account which suppresses them is seriously defective. Similarly, the socialist critic does not see literature in terms of ideology or class-struggle because these happen to be his or her political interests, arbitrarily projected on to literary works. He or she would hold that such matters are the very stuff of history, and that in so far as literature is an historical phenomenon, they are the very stuff of literature too.[1]

It seems reasonable that most critics—and readers in general— look at literature to see how it represents what is most important to them in the world outside of literature. If we could just pin down what is important out there in the world, then everything else in the world, including literature, should be describable in relation to that standard. And although most postmodern critics avoid absolute standards, it remains entirely possible that there is some ultimate standard to judge things by. If, therefore, one makes the Christian claim that the redemptive death of Christ is what is most important in the world, then one should look at literature to see how it represents that pattern of redemption.

---

1. Eagleton, *Literary Theory*, 209.

In simplest form, that is the claim of this book: that all literature expresses, in various forms, a pattern of creation, fall, and redemption. Boiled down yet further, this claim is nothing more than the assertion that in literature something is resolved. Such a simple claim is almost irrefutable, but is also too simplistic to reveal much about literature. My goal in this book will be to define and explain the archetypal pattern of redemption that underlies our whole notion of "resolution" in literature and to demonstrate, through multiple examples, that successful literature—poems and stories that have shown endurance or popularity—uses this pattern in specific ways. Readers who employ this theory should understand particular works of literature and the general notion of literature better than they did before.

Because I emphasize not only redemption but the pattern of redemption that is most typically associated with Christianity, I suspect that many critics will reject this approach out of hand as mere religion in the guise of criticism. However, prior to any claims about this pattern of redemption, I would like to posit one prior assumption that readers of any background or persuasion should be able to accept: literature is about life and death. It may describe moments in lives, real or imaginary. It may trace the narrative course of a life from its past, to a moment of the present, to a projected future. It may present a life or a moment in a life in ways that are realistic or idealized. It may speculate about death—its causes, effects, qualities—exploring what might happen after the end point of a life. I would like to suggest that what makes a given work of literature popular or significant is largely the way in which that work deals with the possible relationships between life and death.

Much of current literary theory ignores relationships between life and death, instead focusing on relationships among words or relationships among people. Those critics who have followed in the tracks of formalistic New Criticism, structuralism, deconstruction, and hermeneutics have focused mainly on relationships among words. In its extreme form, this type of criticism has made the kind of claim that Jacques Derrida makes in *Of Grammatology* when he says, "*There is nothing outside of the text* [there is no outside-text; *il n'y a pas de hors-texte*]. . . . in what one calls the real life of these existences 'of flesh and bone,' beyond and behind what one believes can be circumscribed as [a particular] text, there has never been anything but writing."[2] Admittedly, this is an extreme position, but if texts are artifacts to be analyzed or just the interplay of signifiers and signifieds, then the task of criticism is to reveal how texts create (or fail to create) meaning. On the other hand, those critics who have pursued theory—Marxists, feminists, multiculturalists, postcolonialists, and such—have tended to follow Michel Foucault's view that there is only the interplay of forms of power in this world. In *Discipline and Punish: The Birth of the Prison*, Foucault describes "those mechanisms that transfer the individual imperceptibly from discipline to the law, from deviation to offence," and he ultimately claims, "there is no outside."[3] If texts are merely a part of this system of "discipline" and "deviation," of power and resistance to power (whether economic, gender, cultural, or political power), then the task of criticism is to use literature to reveal this interplay of forms of power. Postmodern thinkers such as Derrida and Foucault generally posit a material world that is a self-contained and self-referential system (or systems). A reading of most postmodern critics and philosophers would suggest that it is now a given that there is no higher reality, no spiritual world—certainly no God—and that there is only this endlessly self-referential, socially constructed web of hegemony and marginalization, of signifiers and signifieds.

However, at least one fact does ultimately lead outside of texts and power systems and outside of the material world: the fact of death. Regardless of one's beliefs and perspectives, it seems inescapable that everyone must die. In *Being and Time*, Martin Heidegger defines death as "the possibility of no-longer-

2. Derrida, *Of Grammatology*, 1825–26.
3. Foucault, *Discipline and Punish*, 1642.

being-able-to-be-there."[4] Heidegger asserts that "Dasein ["being-there," the perceiving existence] becomes 'essentially' Dasein in that authentic existence which constitutes itself as anticipatory resoluteness";[5] and this "resoluteness" seems to be nothing less than an acceptance of the fact of death: "When Dasein is resolute, it takes over authentically in its existence the fact that it is the null basis of its own nullity."[6] In other words, we exist "authentically" when we face the fact of death.

Death exists "outside" of Foucault's system of power because death is outside of all "those mechanisms that transfer the individual imperceptibly from discipline to the law, from deviation to offence." While this system may well include execution, death is what is situated beyond execution. And death escapes from Derrida's "text" because although we have the signifier "death," the signified is "null" (as Heidegger puts it) or at best unknowable.[7] It is ineluctable death that eventually forces every philosophy, every worldview, and every consciousness outside of themselves and into "that unknown country."

Likewise, it is death that opens the possibility of "something after death." If death is pure nullity, then Foucault and Derrida and the postmodern world can claim with impunity that "there is no outside." However—and this is the basis for all my following claims—it cannot be proven that death is nullity. If it is not, if death is a separation or an awakening or a transformation or a transfiguration, then the possibility of a higher, greater, or at least different "reality" opens to us. Heidegger admits this possibility

4. Heidegger, *Being and Time*, 294.

5. Ibid., 370.

6. Ibid., 354.

7. One might be tempted to say that Derrida has already asserted that death—nullity, *nothing*—exists outside of the text: the statement "There is nothing outside of the text" equals "nothing/nullity/death exists outside of the text." The French original will not sustain such an interpretation, lacking any signifier for "nothing," but perhaps Derrida will allow us the play of translation.

in a negative way: "That there are 'eternal truths' will not be adequately proved until someone has succeeded in demonstrating that Dasein has been and will be for all Eternity."[8] His agnosticism toward or even rejection of that which is eternal or essential is typical of postmodern thought. But Heidegger's claim at least posits the possibility that *dasein* (roughly what was once called "the soul") is "going to" an eternal future. Hamlet says the same thing more simply: "in that sleep of death what dreams may come / . . . Must give us pause."[9]

This fact of death opens up questions: What is life? And does life continue in some way after death? Is there some greater power not subject to death, to which even death is subject? Such questions cannot be answered "within the text"—within this contingent, material world. These questions do, however, force us all, sooner or later, to consider death and its relationships to our lives and to find ways to conceptualize, compartmentalize, perhaps even control it. And I will suggest here that most if not all people and cultures try to handle the fact of death through the concept of redemption.

In simplest form, redemption is a pattern of debt and payment or of loss and reclamation. *The American Heritage Dictionary* defines this sort of redemption as "deliverance upon payment of ransom; rescue." Death is loss of this material, contingent life, but perhaps some payment can be made to reclaim that loss. In one way or another, practically everyone searches for some "payment of ransom"—some "rescue"—from death. In some societies, this payment is made through ancestor worship, as a way of ensuring that the dead remain in contact with the world of the living. In other societies, such as ancient Egypt, those who were able sought immortality through elaborate burials and mummification. In contemporary America, increasingly expensive medical procedures offer not only the promise of extended life but the dream of eternal youth: we try to buy our way out of death. Various

8. Ibid., 269–70.

9. Shakespeare, *Hamlet*, III. i. 66, 68.

religions offer various means of redemption. In Hinduism, it is devotion to the gods and living according to one's *dharma*. In Buddhism, it is control of the passions to attain *nirvana*. In Islam, it is obedience to a set of laws. And in Christianity, it is (to cite once again *The American Heritage Dictionary*) "salvation from sin through Christ's sacrifice."

And this brings me to a primary assumption of this book. I will claim not only that the quest for redemption from death is a common, normal, and perhaps even essential component of human thought, but that the ultimate form of such redemption is the one presented in the Christian gospel: the voluntary, sacrificial death of the perfect and innocent redeemer as a ransom for the lives of those who are lost. The presumption here is that death involves loss too great to be redeemed by an animal sacrifice, by a ritual, or by any merely human activity. Consequently, the payment to be made must be as great as or greater than human life. So the redeemer must offer more than an ordinary human life to pay for redemption. Christian doctrine would claim that the loss involved is the fall of humankind: the loss of a perfect love relationship with God due to people's disobedience to God (i.e., sin). The payment for this loss is death (see Rom 3:23; 6:23). A person who has disobeyed God (sinned) cannot redeem himself or herself, so a sinless redeemer is needed. To pay for the sins of all mankind, a divine and sinless redeemer is needed.

With regards to literature, then, I will claim that variations of this Christian redemptive pattern are essential to all poems, plays, and stories. Some works toy with it, repeatedly offering then withdrawing potential acts of redemption. Some deliberately subvert it, creating the effects of horror or meaninglessness by inverting or denying redemption. In many of the most popular and enduring works, a more-or-less Christlike redeemer risks or gives his or her life to redeem someone who is in danger of being lost. As Father Zosima says in Dostoevsky's *The Brothers Karamazov*, "Men are always saved after the death of the deliverer."[10] What really matters in any work of literature is how it deals with loss and redemption.

Although this pattern of redemption from death is presented in the Christian gospel, it is separate from "religion." Religion is, after all, very much inside of Foucault's "mechanisms that transfer the individual imperceptibly from discipline to the law, from deviation to offence." But this redemption is not achieved or granted by any institution. And it is not merely a moral code, a list of rules that people can obey to earn their own redemption. Many religious systems provide moral codes, whether Judeo-Christian, Moslem, Hindu, Buddhist, Shintoist, Taoist, Confucian, or atheist. It is true that literature can be judged by whether it supports or subverts such a moral code. A Marxist moral code might claim that whatever leads toward the communal possession of the means of production is good, and a Marxist critic might praise works of literature that illustrate this code. But this seems to me to be a very limited kind of criticism. It reveals one aspect of human life but not the central issues of life and death. Likewise, one could assert that the Christian moral code is the "Golden Rule," stated by Jesus in Matthew 7:12: "whatever you want men to do to you, do also to them." But a hypothetical Golden-Rule critic cannot ultimately ask much more than, "Are the characters in this story nice people?" This may well be a criterion that some readers value in literature, but again, this seems to me to be very limited criticism, and it does not deal with the ultimate relationship of life and death.

Instead, Christian redemption actually begins from the position that a moral code only presents the ways for people to be lost. The Apostle Paul wrote: "For if there had been a law given which could have given life, truly righteousness would have been by the law. But the Scripture has confined all under sin, that the promise by faith in Jesus Christ might be given to those who believe. But before faith came, we were kept under guard by the law, kept for the faith which would afterward be revealed. Therefore the law was

10. Dostoevsky, *The Brothers Karamazov*, 301.

our tutor to bring us to Christ, that we might be justified by faith" (Gal 3:21b–24). In other words, the "law" exists only to reveal that people are, in a theological sense, lost (see also Rom 3:19; 3:23; Jas 2:10). Being lost is one important element of the structure of literature. And there are, in fact, works of literature that simply illustrate a character's descent into lostness, without reference to redemption: Camus's *L'étranger* or Becket's *Waiting for Godot*, for instance, come to mind.[11] But Christianity claims that there are both a need and a way to be redeemed after violating the moral code and being lost, and I will claim that significant literature typically explores both ways to be lost and ways to be redeemed.

Going further, I wish to claim that Christian redemption corresponds to a universal pattern—an archetype—that is essential to all human thought and behavior. This pattern can be reduced to three terms: creation, fall, and redemption. The first term is common to all religious and philosophical systems. Everyone believes that this world came into existence somehow, whether through divine fiat, cyclical destruction and creation, or random chance. This element need not be Christian in any way since anyone who believes in existence believes in a form of creation. Consequently, this element is important to literary criticism but is not unique to any one theory of criticism. Most readers and critics no doubt assume that good literature reflects the principle of creation by creating its own internal universe. Since the time of Aristotle, *mimesis* has been an important concept in literary studies. Through description and imagery, characterization and dialogue, works of literature must imitate, reflect, or create their own worlds in order to be effective. It is possible that creation is especially important to Christian readers and critics because they generally believe in a divine act of creation that might be reflected by an author's act of literary creation and because the Christian belief in the incarnation of God—the entry of the Divine into creation—might lead

11. Works such as *L'étranger* and *Waiting for Godot* may actually emphasize redemption by portraying its absence.

them to value creation more highly than others. However, even belief in divine incarnation is not unique to Christianity. Ancient Greek gods took on human forms and created semidivine humans by copulating with mortals. Hindu gods such as Vishnu became incarnate in avatars such as Krishna. Perhaps no other religion claims a unique son of a unique God, but incarnation alone is not sufficient to define Christianity, and so this element of creativity will simply be posited in this study as a given: good literature uses language to create in readers a perception of a world.[12]

The second term of the archetypal pattern of redemption is the fall. In Christian theological terms, the fall is the human loss of relationship with God caused by sin: disobedience to God's law (see Rom 3:23; 5:12–19). However, in literature the fall may be much more general and is, in basic terms, a necessity of all plots. Although some lyric poetry might involve mere creation of a scene or state of being, narrative plot requires that something change. An initial state of goodness might be disrupted, or the initial state might already be unacceptable, but unless something is "wrong"— motivating a change in situation or characterization—nothing happens: there is no plot. As Dostoevsky's devil says to Ivan Karamazov, "If everything in the universe were sensible, nothing would happen. There would be no events without [me], and there must be events."[13] In "Structural Analysis of Narrative," Tzvetan Todorov claims that "the minimal complete plot can be seen as the shift from one equilibrium to another. . . . The two moments of equilibrium, similar and different, are separated by a period of imbalance, which is composed of a process of degeneration and a process of improvement."[14] In other words, a plot needs a complication and a resolution. The complication, Todorov's "degeneration," is the literary equivalent of the theological concept of the fall. As

---

12. New Critical close reading typically focuses on this aspect of literature: how language functions to create images in readers.

13. Ibid., 609.

14. Todorov, "Structural Analysis of Narrative," 2105.

with the term of creation, I take this term as so basic and universal to literature that it is a given: at least in narrative forms, literature must include some sort of fall.

The third and most significant term of this redemptive pattern can be expressed by various theological words and phrases: redemption, justification, salvation, eternal life. In simple terms, it says that people who are wrong, lost, in danger, even dead are made right, safe, and alive by the work of the incarnate son of God. John 3:16 says, "For God so loved the world that He gave His only begotten Son, that whoever believes in Him should not perish, but have everlasting life." And the Apostle Paul says in 1 Corinthians, "I declare to you the gospel . . . by which also you are saved . . . : that Christ died for our sins according to the Scriptures" (15:1–3). Christian theology claims that all people are subject to eternal death because of the effects of sin (Rom 3:23; 6:23). Jesus offered his perfect, divine life to redeem lost, sinful people from sin. Jesus himself said, "the Son of Man has come to seek and to save that which was lost" (Luke 19:10), and "the Son of Man did not come to be served, but to serve, and to give His life a ransom for many" (Mark 10:45). Jesus the redeemer is the central and unique figure of Christianity. More recently, C. S. Lewis put it this way: "The central Christian belief is that Christ's death has somehow put us right with God and given us a fresh start."[15]

This is not to claim, however, that the concept of redemption is only found in Christianity. On the contrary, I am arguing that redemption is central to human ways of dealing with the reality of death. Consequently, it is found in other, imperfect forms throughout human beliefs and activities, across cultures and historical epochs. Missionary and author Don Richardson calls these imperfect forms "redemptive analogies."[16] He claims that even in times and places where Christianity has been unknown, people have expressed their deeply felt need of redemption. From primitive sacrifices of

15. Lewis, *Mere Christianity*, 57.
16. Richardson, *Peace Child*, 288.

chickens to the postmodern drive to oppose oppressive systems, people understand that there must be sacrifice to overcome evil. We can see this concept in Job, who could say long before the time of Jesus, "For I know that my Redeemer lives, and He shall stand at last on the earth; and after my skin is destroyed, this I know, that in my flesh I shall see God" (Job 19:25–26). We can see the same deep feeling in the Japanese kamikaze warrior who willingly laid down his life to defend his homeland or the firefighter who rushes into a burning building to save a child. People know or feel that sacrifice is necessary to save/rescue/redeem those who are lost.

Therefore, I propose that this pattern of divine redemption—sacrifice to bring wholeness—is the most important archetype not just in Christianity, but in life. I further propose that when we turn to literature, this is the pattern that ultimately determines how readers respond to literature. Though audiences may not be conscious of the presence of redemptive patterns, their deeply felt responses to the presence or absence of redemption are what ultimately determine their responses to a given work of literature. I will also suggest that redemptive patterns influence responses to every level of literary structure, from plot and character to setting and even word choice. In short, redemption is the essence of literature.

As mentioned above, in its simplest form, this claim that redemption is central to literature can be reduced to the claim that a story must have a plot. If we see Todorov's "imbalance"/complication as a "fall"—a loss of an original state of goodness—and his second "equilibrium"/resolution as a restoration of that state of goodness, we need only look for the action that "pays" for that restoration and we will have found a basic pattern of redemption. However, I want to go beyond such a basic claim to propose that the more closely this plot resolution follows the Christian pattern of innocent and intentional sacrifice to bring salvation, the more powerfully readers tend to respond to the work of literature. In other words, the greater the danger or loss and the greater the sacrifice to redeem it, the more popular and/or emotionally powerful the literature will be. In particular, the redeemer must be willing to sacrifice his or her own life to save another. The redeemer who offers mere money or labor is not as great as the one who gives life. The one who saves himself or herself is not as great as the one who saves another. And the unwilling or unintentional redeemer is not as great as the one who voluntarily offers his or her life. In subsequent chapters, I will examine some of the world's most enduring or best-selling works of literature to show how they illustrate this principle.

One way to see how variations on the pattern of redemption affect readers' responses is by looking at traditional genres of literature. Some genres seem to be valued more highly than others because of the ways that they conform or fail to conform to the pattern. For instance, while farce is popular, few people would claim that it is the greatest form of literature. The essence of farce is harm or error: someone is hurt or makes a mistake. This might be considered as a form of sin or fallenness: the condition that requires redemption. But there is no redeemer. The Marx brothers never lay down their lives for another. There is no redeeming sacrifice in a Monty Python skit. If there is redemption, it is the redemption that comes from the audience's recognition that the harm is not real, the error can be fixed. This recognition brings laughter. Therefore, the audience's laughter may function as the redeeming factor in farce. If no one laughs, the farce is a failure: the audience feels only pain or shame. Great literature may contain farce, especially as an element to reveal man's lost state—think of the gravedigger in *Hamlet*. But farce, by itself, cannot rise to the level of the greatest literature.

As a somewhat "higher" genre (in most people's estimation), comedy is also popular, but sometimes attains a degree of recognition as great art. I believe that this is because it is at least partially founded on redemption. In comedy, the plot complication—the "fall" of some character—may be resolved by a good deed or by good fortune, but it requires effort. The lovers are united in *A Midsummer Night's Dream* because Oberon's magic and Puck's meddling set everything right. No sacrificial death is needed to bring this redemption, but there is at least difficulty or struggle. In *Pride and Prejudice*, Elizabeth and Darcy are finally united after various plot twists and misunderstandings when they admit their own weaknesses and misconceptions and make themselves open to personal change. In the first Star Wars movie (Part 4: *A New Hope*), Darth Vader and "the dark side" are defeated by the heroic struggles of Luke Skywalker, Han Solo, and Princess Leia, but no major character dies to bring this redemption. However, this example leads on to a greater kind of redemption. When the entire sextology is considered, Obi-Wan Kenobi becomes a more significant character, so his death in Part 4 can be interpreted as a redeeming sacrifice that enables Luke to overcome the dark side. Furthermore, the centrality of Anakin Skywalker/Darth Vader in the entire series makes his ultimate repentant death and transformation into an act that begins to resemble the pattern of death of a redeemer to bring salvation. One could argue that, taken as the story of Anakin Skywalker, the Star Wars series can be interpreted as a tragedy.

It is the genre of tragedy that provides the best evidence of the centrality of redemption in literature. Tragedy has often been considered the highest form of literature, and I argue that this estimation has arisen precisely because this genre most often approaches the Christian pattern of redemption. The noble tragic hero attains some goal of cleansing or salvation through his or her self-sacrifice. Oedipus is great not because he merely learns who he is and suffers, but because his suffering brings cleansing. He has both paid for his own sins and saved Thebes from a plague. Likewise, Hamlet is great not because he kills Claudius but because he comes to a realization that his fallen state can be overcome: "the readiness is all." At his death, the state of Denmark is cleansed of its rottenness, and there is hope for a new, clean beginning. Without these transformations in Oedipus and Hamlet and in their homelands, their ends would be mere acts of violence. Oedipus and Hamlet are not Christ figures. They are neither divine nor innocent. They do not willingly lay down their lives. But their greatness lies in the degree to which they approximate the role of the redeemer. And audiences feel the greatness of these stories because they feel the depth of the redemptive analogy.

In the following chapters, I will explore various works of literature to see how they employ the redemptive scheme. In chapter 2, I compare Shakespeare's *Hamlet* and *Coriolanus* to explore how the use of redemption makes one work greater than the other. I also analyze the redemptive patterns of pre-Christian classics such as *Oedipus the King*, the *Iliad*, the *Odyssey*, and *Śakuntala*. Chapter 3 examines best-selling literature from around the world to reveal connections between redemption and popularity. Chapters 4 and 5 present the deliberate inversion of redemption that creates the genre of the horror story and the mocking or frustration of redemption typical of postmodern and postcolonial literature. In chapter 6, I attempt to work out how the redemptive pattern functions not only at the level of narrative plot, but even in the structures of lyric poetry and in the most basic linguistic level of all: the sentence. By examining classics and popular works from a variety of both Christian and non-Christian cultures, I hope to show that the effectiveness of literature and of language itself comes from variations on the pattern of redemption. Literature's popularity and greatness can be determined by how well it creates its own world, how great a loss is at stake in that world, and ultimately how great a sacrifice redeems that loss.

# 2

## Testing the Theory

IF REDEMPTION is the ultimate pattern that we seek in literature, a comparison of various works of similar genre by the same author should help to reveal the effects of this pattern. For example, Shakespeare's *The Tragedy of Hamlet, Prince of Denmark* is widely considered one of the world's greatest dramas, while *The Tragedy of Coriolanus*, written a few years later, is generally accepted to be a lesser work. Why? It can be argued that Hamlet is a more complex character than Coriolanus or that the poetry of the latter play is inferior. These are factors in the creativity of the play. But even so, one wonders why the mature Shakespeare would write less effectively for one than for the other. Perhaps he wrote in a hurry or had emotional distractions, or some such personal explanation that can no longer be demonstrated. However, I would argue that a key—probably the key—to the weakness of *Coriolanus* is that, unlike *Hamlet*, the protagonist is not portrayed as an innocent redeemer and the plot is not a story of redemption.

### THE TRAGEDY OF CORIOLANUS

Coriolanus is not an innocent redeemer. He is a warrior of great courage, given to anger, impatience, and blunt disdain for the lower classes. He is noble by birth and portrayed as a man of noble courage. Otherwise, however, he is scarcely admirable. After a great victory in battle, Coriolanus is asked to go before the plebeians to ask for their votes to make him consul. He does this with such bad grace as to be offensive. After meeting several commoners, he says:

> Better it is to die, better to starve,
> Than crave the hire which first we do deserve.
> Why in this woolvish toge should I stand here,
> To beg of Hob and Dick that does appear
> Their needless vouches?[1]

When they react to his comments by revoking their votes for him, an uprising ensues, and Coriolanus's friends beg him to calm the mob by flattering them. At first he refuses, until even his mother tells him, "Thy valiantness was mine, thou suck'st it from me, / But owe thy pride thyself" (III. ii. 128–29). Finally, he agrees and promises to flatter the people and speak "mildly." In spite of repeated promises, however, as soon as an accusation is made against him, he replies, "The fires i' th' lowest hell fold in the people!" (III. iii. 68). He seems incapable of civil behavior, even when it is manifestly in his own best interest. As a result of his own willful offensiveness, he is banished. Although various characters in the play assert that he is noble, his words and actions, outside of his courage in battle, are mostly obnoxious, so his "tragic fall" seems largely deserved.

More importantly, Coriolanus is not a redeemer. After the plebians force his exile from Rome, he joins with his archenemy, Aufidius the Volscian, to attack Rome. With the city at his feet, his wife, son, and mother plead with him to show mercy, and he gives in. This could have been a redemptive climax: Coriolanus could have forgiven those who exiled him and laid down his life for his family and nation. By doing so, he might have approached the pattern of the innocent redeemer laying down his life to save others. But instead there is only the slightest hint of redemption. He briefly recognizes the possibility that he might suffer to save Rome:

1. Shakespeare, *Coriolanus*, II. iii. 115–19.

> . . . O my mother! O!
> You have won a happy victory to Rome;
> But, for your son—believe it. O, believe it!—
> Most dangerously you have with him prevailed,
> If not most mortal to him. (V. iii. 185–89)

However, this is not a clear act of redemption. Rome is spared but remains under the corrupt and fickle power of the tribunes and the mob. Coriolanus does not forgive: he merely decides that his mother is right and that he should not destroy his own family. There is just a hint of self-sacrifice when he says here that his decision not to destroy Rome could be dangerous to himself, but when he returns to the Volscians, he seems to expect them to receive him and accept his decision to spare Rome. He tells the Volscian leaders:

> Hail, lords! I am returned your soldier;
> No more infected with my country's love
> Than when I parted hence, but still subsisting
> Under your great command. (V. vi. 70–73)

He is outraged when Aufidius turns against him, and he dies boasting about his military prowess:

> Cut me to pieces, Volsces, men and lads,
> Stain all your edges on me. "Boy"! False hound!
> If you have writ your annals true, 'tis there,
> That, like an eagle in a dovecote, I
> Fluttered your Volscians in Corioles.
> Alone I did it. (V. vi. 110–15)

There is no sense here of saving another or even himself. Coriolanus shows rage and pride. So Rome is spared but not restored to goodness, and Coriolanus is killed without sacrifice or restoration. The loss of Coriolanus redeems nothing and no one. Without redemption, the play probably leaves most audiences feeling frustration and emptiness.

## THE TRAGEDY OF HAMLET, PRINCE OF DENMARK

*Hamlet* could have been a similar story, with a guilty protagonist and a lack of redemption, but instead it turns a simple act of revenge into a redeeming sacrifice. The protagonist does some despicable things: killing Polonius, rejecting Ophelia and driving her insane, and manipulating the execution of his friends Rosencrantz and Guildenstern. However, in the structure of the play, he is portrayed as largely innocent. Claudius's act of murder and the ghost's supernatural imposition of the task of revenge place Hamlet in a position where he must feign madness and use violence both to defend himself and to accomplish his destined task. And he repeatedly shows a sensitivity that humanizes and, in a sense, purifies him. For example, after he "accidentally" kills Polonius, he says, "For this same lord, / I do repent; but heaven hath pleased it so, / To punish me with this, and this with me."[2] Coriolanus never reveals such a conscience. And Hamlet's intentions always seem good. As he tells Gertrude, "I must be cruel only to be kind" (III. iv. 179).

Furthermore, Hamlet's actions go beyond mere revenge. He could have justly executed Claudius at the play-within-the-play, at prayer in the chapel, even at Ophelia's grave, and then defended the rightness of his actions. In consequence, he might have been executed as a criminal or lived on as king of Denmark. Audiences might have been satisfied, but they would not have been awed. What makes *Hamlet* a great play, if my principle of interpretation is correct, is that Hamlet recognizes that "Something is rotten in the State of Denmark" (I. iv. 90) and that he was "born to set it right" (I. v. 189). He considers his own mortality and finally concludes that "there is a special providence" (V. ii. 221–22) that directs all things and that "the readiness is all" (V. ii. 224). As a result, when he does finally kill Claudius, we feel that he has restored right order in Elsinore. In fact, in his final speech, he is concerned with re-establishing proper rule in the kingdom (V. ii. 357–60). However,

2. Shakespeare, *Hamlet*, III. iv. 173–75.

this new order is established at a terrible cost so that when Hamlet finally says, "the rest is silence" (V. ii. 360), we feel that he has died in some sense as a sacrificial victim. Unlike Coriolanus, he sacrifices himself in order to set things right.

It can be argued that this is simply the nature of true tragedy. The tragic hero must be partly good (Aristotle would say "noble") and must achieve something through his fall. But I would argue that there is a greater principle at work here: that true tragedy is effective precisely because it is a pattern that incorporates an element of redemption. The hero who dies for nothing is merely pathetic. On the other hand, an evil protagonist who falls gets simple justice. In *Macbeth* or *Richard III*, for instance, unless the audience believes there is some redeeming goodness in the protagonist, they experience his death at the conclusion of the play as good and just but not tragic.[3] But the true tragic hero, the noble character who sacrifices him- or herself to achieve something good, is at least partially a redeemer.

## OEDIPUS THE KING

Consider another tragic hero. *Oedipus the King* is a key example supporting my claims because it comes from a non-Christian culture. Redemption in any literature coming from a Christian culture could be seen as the outcome of cultural assumptions originating in Christianity rather than as something essentially human. In Western literature after the first century, patterns of redemption might appear because of a deliberate desire to recreate the story of Christ. In the Arthurian Grail quests, in Dante's *Comedia*, in *Don Quixote*, *Faust*, *Les Miserables*, and *Huckleberry Finn*, the pattern of redemption is obvious but may be deliberate. However, Sophocles was not influenced by the Gospels. If the

3. It can be argued that Macbeth is tragic primarily because the audience normally perceives Macbeth as deceived by the prophecies of the Weird Sisters and manipulated by his wife's ambitions and so not wholly at fault for his evil deeds.

redeemer is the central figure in all of literature (I would say, in all of life), this claim must be supported not only by literature from Christian cultures but by non-Christian literature as well. If Christian criticism is "the real thing"—the best and most useful approach to interpretation of literature—then it must explain the effectiveness of any story, poem, or play, not just works that openly espouse the Christian faith.

Thus, *Oedipus the King* is a test case. It fits, first of all, because there is a clearly defined fall. At the start of the play, Thebes is suffering:

> A blight is on the fruitful plants of the earth,
> a blight is on the cattle in the fields,
> a blight is on our women that no children
> are born to them; a God that carries fire,
> a deadly pestilence, is on our town,
> strikes us and spares not . . .[4]

Next, there is a clearly defined need for redemption. The people come to Oedipus expecting him to save them: "For this land of ours / calls you its savior since you saved it once" (47–48). And Oedipus himself claims the role of savior, saying, "Indeed I'm willing to give all / that you may need" (11–12) and "may I prove a villain, / if I shall not do all the God commands" (76–77). When the oracle of Apollo announces how to save Thebes, the solution is not only given in religious terms—"drive out a pollution from our land" (97)—but in redemptive terms: "expiation / of blood by blood" (100–01). And when Oedipus calls on Teiresias to explain how to carry out Apollo's command, he says, "save yourself and the city, / save me; redeem the debt of our pollution" (312–13).[5] Teiresias then tries to show Oedipus that despite the "luck" that enabled him to save Thebes earlier from the Sphinx, he is now

---

4. Sophocles *Oedipus* 25–30; references are to lines.

5. The word translated "redeem," *rhusai,* meaning rescue, save, or deliver, is actually used three times in these two lines.

the cause of the problem and will be destroyed by his own "luck." Oedipus replies, "I do not care, if it has saved this city" (443).

Finally, Oedipus suffers to save Thebes. He says, "Now I am found to be / a sinner and a son of sinners" (1397–98), and he begs Creon, "Drive me from here with all the speed you can / to where I may not hear a human voice" (1436–37). When Oedipus blinds himself and departs into exile, he has not only avenged his father's death and learned who he is, but he also has saved Thebes. The gods were punishing Thebes for harboring sin. Oedipus sacrifices his family, his kingship, and his eyesight in expiation of his own sins and as the redeemer of his city. Audiences feel that *Oedipus the King* is not just a murder mystery full of sexual perversion, but an exploration of the kind of sacrifice needed to heal and restore a fallen world.

It is true that this play is not purely about the redemption of Thebes. As the plot progresses, it becomes more and more about Oedipus himself and his discovery of his own fallenness, as killer of his father and husband of his mother. In fact, much of the effect of the play comes from the lack of redemption for Oedipus himself. In chapter 4, I will explore works based on a pattern of antiredemption and how they create the effect of horror. *Coriolanus*, *Hamlet*, and *Oedipus the King* all contain elements of this horror caused by a failure of redemption. Nevertheless, I believe it is clear that both *Hamlet* and *Oedipus the King* rise above the level of even the best horror stories because they combine the level of personal loss with another level where loss and suffering leads to redemption.

## THE *ILIAD*

As further examples of pre-Christian literature, the *Iliad* and *Odyssey* should be good test cases for redemption criticism because they obviously could not have been influenced by Christian writings. Because they have remained popular across time and various cultures, they must be considered significant literature. It is probably still true, as Walter Miller claims in the introduction to his 1945 translation, that "apart from the most ancient books of the Bible the oldest piece of literature of general interest to us and our civilization is the *Iliad* of Homer."[6] So the question is what makes them significant? I will argue that their significance comes from their use of the pattern of creation, fall, and ultimate redemption.

Looking first at the *Iliad*, it uses creation in several ways. First, it obviously uses language to create an imaginative world that combines the realistic with the mythic. For example, almost immediately after the epic invocation,[7] Homer creates a picture, with dialogue, of a father pleading for the release of his captive daughter while calling upon the gods to intervene in the world. Chryses, the priest of Apollo, addresses Agamemnon and Menelaos:

> Sons of Atreus and you other strong-greaved Achaians,
> to you may the gods grant who have their homes on Olympos
> Priam's city to be plundered and a fair homecoming thereafter,
> but may you give me back my own daughter and take the ransom,
> giving honor to Zeus' son who strikes from afar, Apollo. (1. 17–21)

The text here combines a very believable character with a supernatural world, a creative pattern that continues throughout the narrative.

Second, the *Iliad* uses creation in the more specific form of divine incarnation. Throughout the *Iliad*, gods frequently appear in human form. Apollo, Ares, Athene, and Poseidon actually fight in battles, sometimes in the form of known people, sometimes in their own persons. In book 5, Diomedes wounds Aphrodite and, with Athene's material help, wounds Ares. In book 13 Poseidon takes on the form of the Achaian augur Kalchas and motivates the Achaians to resist Hektor. In book 17, Athena takes the form of the Achaian Phoinix to encourage Menelaos, while Apollo takes the forms of the Trojans Periphas, Asios, and Phainops to encourage Aineias and Hektor. Such incarnations are partly a reflection

6. W. Miller, Introduction, x.
7. Homer *Iliad* 1.1–7.

of the anthropomorphism of ancient Greek polytheism. However, as a literary device, they give the story superhuman significance. Because this story brings divinities into the human sphere, readers feel that the action transcends what is merely human.

Another element of incarnation works in the other direction, as human characters are raised to the level of the divine. This is most apparent in the *Iliad* in that the main character, Achilleus, is the child of the goddess Thetis, and her advocacy of her son drives much of the action. He seems to be a near equal of the gods. Minor characters such as Helen, Aineias, and Sarpedon are also presented as offspring of deities. One might argue that heroes, by definition, are always perceived to transcend human nature in some way. But this claim actually strengthens the position of Christian criticism as the best method of literary analysis because Christian assumptions about reality explain why heroic characters from Achilleus to Hugo's Jean Valjean to Achebe's Okonkwo have tended to dominate great literature. If incarnation is one of the ultimate themes of life and literature, then readers will be drawn to characters who, by their grand heroic nature or actions, seem in some way to incarnate divinity.

The most obvious fall in the story of the *Iliad* appears when, after nine years of stalemate, the stasis of the war is upset when Agamemnon (Atreus's son) offends Achilleus, who withdraws from the Achaian ranks. The well-known epic invocation identifies this central conflict:

> Sing, goddess, the anger of Peleus' son Achilleus
> and its devastation, which put pains thousandfold upon the Achaians,
> hurled in their multitudes to the house of Hades strong souls
> of heroes, but gave their bodies to be the delicate feasting
> of dogs, of all birds, and the will of Zeus was accomplished
> since that time when first there stood in division of conflict
> Atreus' son the lord of men and brilliant Achilleus. (1. 1–7)

Thus, the opening of the poem focuses on the anger (one could call it the sin) that produces alienation, separation, and ultimately destruction among the Achaian army. The claim that "souls" are hurled into "Hades" and that the action all follows "the will of Zeus" gives the story a spiritual setting that implies a need for redemption from the outset.

Next, before taking up Agamemnon's offense against Achilleus, Homer presents Agamemnon's offense against the god Apollo. The Achaian king had captured the daughter of Chryses, the priest of Apollo, and refused to return her to Chryses even though he came, as related above, "to ransom / back his daughter, carrying gifts beyond count and holding" (1. 12–13). Here the theme of ransom/redemption is emphasized, and Agamemnon's refusal to allow redemption leads to a terrible plague from Apollo. The prophet Kalchas claims that Agamemnon must return the girl, along with an offering to Apollo, saying, "we might propitiate and persuade him" (1. 69, 100). When Achilleus supports Kalchas and demands that Agamemnon return the girl to her father, along with "a sacred hecatomb / for the god" (1. 447–48), Agamemnon demands that he receive compensation from Achilleus. He takes Achilleus's war prize, the maiden Briseis, and Achilleus's wrath is thereby aroused. This wrath is given supernatural force when Achilleus's goddess/mother Thetis begs Zeus to justify her son by allowing the Achaian forces to suffer defeat until Agamemnon repents and reconciles with Achilleus. Clearly, offense and redemption are the central themes presented in book 1 of the *Iliad*.

Ultimately then, in the pattern of creation, fall, and redemption, Homer uses redemption as the foundation for his story. If the *Iliad* were a simple tale of winning and losing a battle, it probably would not have survived as great literature but as an obscure ancient saga. It is true that much of the bulk of the epic comes from fairly predictable accounts of one warrior challenging and battling another. Books 4, 5, 7, 8, 11, 12, 13, 15, and large portions of several others consist mostly of accounts of who kills or wounds whom. But the *Iliad* is not primarily about stabbing and hacking but about "the anger of . . . Achilleus" and how that anger is ultimately appeased.

In the end, the death of an innocent savior brings redemption and reconciliation. In book 9, the aged counselor Nestor urges Agamemnon to "think how we can make this good and persuade" Achilleus, and Agamemnon does repent and offer "to make all good, and give back gifts in abundance" (9. 112, 120). He offers to return Briseis to Achilleus along with extravagant redemptive gifts, but Achilleus refuses to be reconciled. Later, in book 16, Achilleus allows his closest friend, Patroklos, to go fight in his stead. As he does so, he prays to Zeus:

> ". . . I myself am staying where the ships are assembled,
> but I send out my companion and many Myrmidons with him
> to fight. Let glory, Zeus of the wide brows, go forth with him.
> ...........................................................................
> then let him come back to me and the running ships, unwounded,
> with all his armour and with the companions who fight close beside
> him."
>     So he spoke in prayer, and Zeus of the counsels heard him.
> The Father granted him one prayer, and denied him the other.
> That Patroklos should beat back the fighting assault on the vessels
> he allowed, but refused to let him come back safe out of the fighting.
> (16. 239–41, 247–52)

Thus, Patroklos goes in a substitutionary role, even wearing Achilleus's armor. He takes Achilleus's place in the battle and temporarily saves the Achaian army. But only after he dies does a full reconciliation occur. After Patroklos has driven back the Trojan army and then been killed by Hektor, Achilleus finally forgives Agamemnon and saves the Achaian army.

Achilleus's forgiveness is not perfect Christian forgiveness: it is based more on vengeance against Hektor, who killed Patroklos, than on pure redemption. But even in his desire for vengeance, he says that Hektor must be killed "and pay the price for stripping Patroklos" (18. 93). In a sense then, Hektor's death also will become a redemptive act. With regard to Agamemnon's offense, Achilleus simply says, "we will let all this be a thing of the past" (18. 112). Later, in book 19, Achilleus addresses Agamemnon and says:

> Son of Atreus, was this after all the better way for
> both, for you and me, that we, for all our hearts' sorrow,
> quarreled together for the sake of a girl in soul-perishing hatred?
> ...............................................................................
> Still we will let all this be a thing of the past, though it hurts us,
> and beat down by constraint the anger that rises inside us.
> Now I am making an end of my anger. It does not become me
> unrelentingly to rage on. (19. 56–58, 65–68)

Thus, in the structure of the *Iliad*, it is the death of the heroic and innocent Patroklos that brings redemption of Achilleus's wrath and salvation of the lost Achaians.

The final books emphasize the atoning value of death. Book 23 relates the funeral and funerary games that Achilleus gives for Patroklos, motivated by the appearance of Patroklos's spirit to the sleeping Achilleus. This appearance is not a full-blown scene of Christlike resurrection, but it does move Achilleus toward a final resolution of his grief, as he says to the spirit, "let us, if only for a little, / embrace and take full satisfaction from the dirge of sorrow" (23. 97–98). In book 24, the final note of the story is the reconciliation of the Trojan king Priam with Achilleus that occurs when the gods enable Priam to redeem Hektor's corpse from Achilleus. Thus, from beginning to end, the *Iliad* is a story of redemption.

## THE *ODYSSEY*

Although a very different kind of story, the *Odyssey* also uses creation, fall, and redemption as key devices and themes. If the story were merely an account of Odysseus's travels, it would probably be remembered, if at all, as a picaresque tale of mythic adventures. But only four of the twenty-four books (books 9 through 12) are primarily about his travels. Instead, the book begins with Odysseus trapped on Kalypso's island, separated from his home and wife, lost, and in need of salvation. And books 1 through 4, sometimes called the "Telemachy," deal mainly with the struggle of Odysseus's son Telemachos to save his mother Penelope, his home, and his patrimony from his mother's suitors. Thus, the *Odyssey* opens with a family disrupted, endangered, in need of redemption, and the story works out this redemption through the characters' personal struggles, the intervention of the gods, and the sacrificial loss of companions.

Beyond the imaginative creation of a mythic world, the *Odyssey* uses incarnational creation focused on Athene, who frequently appears in human form, sometimes as a known character (such as Nestor), sometimes in her own person. She appears in human form in books 1, 2, 7, 8, 13, 15, 16, 22, and 24. Most of Odysseus's traveling is motivated by his interactions with her and with Poseidon. There is little of the use of demigods like Achilleus or Aineias in the *Odyssey*, but the protagonist interacts quite carnally with two minor deities, Circe and Kalypso, and he is often referred to as "godlike Odysseus." Thus Odysseus, almost as much as Achilleus, is portrayed as a near equal of the gods. Like the *Iliad*, this story uses incarnation to bring the realm of the divine into the human sphere and make readers feel that the action transcends the merely human.

The fall underlying the *Odyssey* is the broken relationship between Odysseus and the god Poseidon. The cause of the "pains he suffered" is specified later in book 1 when Zeus explains to Athene that "It is the Earth Encircler Poseidon who, ever relentless, / nurses a grudge because of the Cyclops, whose eye he [Odysseus] blinded."[8]

Odysseus "sinned" against Poseidon by harming the god's son. The results of this sin are ten extra years of separation from his family and, ultimately, the death of all Odysseus's men. He finally is allowed to reach home because of the intercession and aid of Athene, but his reconciliation with the god Poseidon is only implied as coming after the story, when Odysseus must go far inland

8. Homer *Odyssey* 1.68–69.

(where his oar is mistaken for a winnowing fan) and there make special sacrifices to Poseidon.[9]

Odysseus is not the only character in need of redemption. When his son Telemachos first appears, Athene has just incarnated herself as Mentes and arrives at Ithaka to find him:

> as he sat among the suitors, his heart deep grieving within him,
> imagining in his mind his great father, how he might come back
> and all throughout the house might cause the suitors to scatter,
> and hold his rightful place and be lord of his own possessions.
> (1. 114–17)

Telemachos grieves over the state of his family and his father's estate and imagines his father as the savior/redeemer. Telemachos has not offended a god and does not suffer as his father does, but like his father, he undertakes a journey and is ultimately saved from death (at the suitors' hands) by Athene (books 1–4 and 15). His sin and his redemption are not as great as his father's, but his home is lost and restored in parallel with his father.

Both Odysseus and Telemachos face alienation and loss and search for personal and family redemption. However, in the popular mind, the *Odyssey* is not primarily about Odysseus's struggle with the god Poseidon or Telemachos's struggle with the suitors, but about Odysseus's travels. Yet even so, the pattern of redemption repeatedly surfaces in the episodes of his travels. In his account to the Phaiakians of his voyages, Odysseus's first adventure is his raid on the Kikonians. He is clearly the aggressor here, but when the Kikonians regroup and threaten to overwhelm his forces, he reveals the pattern—to be repeated often—of escaping with loss: "and out of each ship six of my strong-greaved companions / were killed, but the rest of us fled away from death and destruction" (9. 60–61). This is hardly the Christian pattern of redemption, but it does begin a series of episodes of salvation purchased by loss of life.

Shortly after this episode, however, comes the key confrontation with Polyphemos, the Cyclops. This story takes most of book 9

---

9. See books 11.121–34 and 23.266–81.

and is the direct cause of Odysseus's "sin" against Poseidon. Trapped in the cave of the cannibal giant Polyphemos, Odysseus relies on himself: "trying to find some release from death, for my companions / and myself too, combining all my resources and treacheries, / as with life at stake" (9. 421–23). However, for all his cleverness, Odysseus survives only because Polyphemos devours four of his companions first—even promising at one point to eat all the others before Odysseus (who has used the pseudonym Nobody): "Then I will eat Nobody after his friends, and the others / I will eat first, and that shall be my guest present to you" (9. 369–70). When he leaves the land of the Cyclopses, he says, "From there we sailed on further along, glad to have escaped death, / but grieving still at heart for the loss of our dear companions" (9. 565–66). So his life is redeemed by the sacrifice of his friends.

The same pattern recurs several times. For example, after his escape from the Laistrygones, he says "From there we sailed on further along, glad to have escaped death, / but grieving still at heart for the loss of our dear companions" (10. 133–34). Likewise, in book 10, one crewman, Elpenor, dies as Odysseus leaves Circe ("I did not lead away my companions without some / loss" 10. 551–52). And in book 12, Odysseus escapes the monster Skylla at the cost of six of his crew (12. 245–59). Ultimately, the entire crew perishes, struck by Zeus's thunderbolts because they had eaten Helios's sacred cattle, and only Odysseus is spared (12. 397–420). Not all of these deaths are redemptive, but a pattern is established that Odysseus lives while others die.

Yet perhaps the most interesting act of redemption in the *Odyssey* is found in book 11, where Odysseus himself experiences a kind of death and resurrection. In book 10, Circe tells him that before he can return home, he must accomplish a journey to Hades to consult with the dead prophet Teiresias. Book 11 covers this journey to the underworld. Odysseus encounters many dead spirits, including his mother, Agamemnon, and Achilleus. The spirit of Teiresias foretells what he must go through to return home. But ironically, this voyage seems completely unnecessary because when Odysseus returns to Circe's island after his journey to the dead, she tells him the same information that Teiresias told him (12. 115–41). Before she does so, she greets him and his crew, saying:

> Unhappy men, who went alive to the house of Hades,
> so dying twice, when all the rest of mankind die only
> once . . .
> ............................................................
> . . . I will show you the way and make plain
> all details, so that neither by land nor on the salt water
> you may suffer and come to grief by unhappy bad designing.
> (12. 21–27)

So it seems that he needed to go to Hades not for the information but because his own symbolic death and return from the dead is an essential part of his redemption.

If this resurrection makes Odysseus into a Christ figure, it is a curious coincidence that when he returns to Ithaka, the old servants Eurykleia, Eumaios, and Philiotios recognize him by his scar (19. 386–94, 21. 217–25). I do not claim, of course, that Homer deliberately foreshadows the Christian gospel. But it might be significant that a redeemer is recognized by his marks of suffering.

Finally, Odysseus returns to redeem his home. In book 22, Odysseus slaughters the suitors who consumed his goods and tried to take his wife. This is not Christian redemption, but vengeance. When one of the suitors, named Eurymachos, offers to pay for the damages done to Odysseus, he responds:

> Eurymachos, if you gave me all your father's possessions,
> all that you have now, and what you could add from elsewhere,
> even so, I would not stay my hands from the slaughter,
> until I had taken revenge for all the suitors' transgression. (22. 61–64)

Therefore, the *Odyssey* is not by any means a Christian story. Redemption in the *Odyssey* is even further from Christian redemption than it is in the *Iliad*, with little emphasis given to innocent victims and with a final redemption that is based on vengeance much more than forgiveness. Nevertheless, this is a story of a fragmented and suffering family restored to wholeness through loss. The invocation in book 1 says:

> Many the pains he suffered in his spirit on the wide sea,
> struggling for his own life and the homecoming of his companions.
> Even so he could not save his companions, hard though
> he strove to . . . (1. 4–7)

Odysseus "could not save his companions," but in the end he is saved himself. This is a story that draws its significance from the repeated use of the pattern of redemptive death. It ends with Athene, incarnate as Mentor, restoring peace between the suitors' families and Odysseus's family. It is a great story because it shows how sin, alienation, and loss can ultimately be redeemed through incarnation and sacrificial suffering and death.

## ŚAKUNTALA AND THE RING OF RECOLLECTION

Another well-known work from outside the Christian tradition is the classical Indian play *Śakuntala*, by the fourth- and fifth-century author Kalidasa. The structure of this play is clearly comic, with separated lovers reunited after difficulties and suffering. Because it is comic, one does not expect to find the death of an innocent redeemer. Nevertheless, this play does show a definite awareness of the need for redemption.

The theme of creation appears in several forms throughout the play. Act 1 begins with a brief hymn on creation and on the creator god Śiva. The action then begins in an Edenic setting with the protagonist, King Dusyanta, entering a forest to hunt an antelope, which he soon learns belongs to the hermitage of a holy sage named Kanva. Monks from this hermitage tell Dusyanta that his bow "should rescue victims, not destroy the innocent."[10] Thus Dusyanta is defined from the outset as a potential savior. The world of the play then moves from the natural world of the forest

10. Kalidasa, "Śakuntala," 754.

and hermitage to the artificial world of the king's court and ultimately to a divine world where Dusyanta goes to war on behalf of the god Indra. As in Homer, the human and the divine interact in this created world.

This world, however, is fallen. The monks from the hermitage ask Dusyanta to stay and protect them from demons that are harassing them while the sage Kanva is away. While he is there, he falls in love with Kanva's beautiful young ward Śakuntala, who is of divine descent. She likewise falls in love with him, and they are secretly married. He returns to his court promising to send for her, but in her lovesickness, she fails to give proper hospitality to a visiting sage, who then curses her:

> Since you blindly ignore
> A great sage like me,
> The lover you worship
> With mindless devotion
> Will not remember you,
> Even when awakened—
> Like a drunkard who forgets
> A story he just composed! (774)

Because of this curse, Dusyanta cannot remember Śakuntala when she arrives at his court pregnant with his only son. She possesses a ring that would restore his memory, but upon realizing that it has slipped off her finger, she exclaims, "I'm lost" (787). Disgraced and unable to return home, she is rescued when "a ray of light in the shape of a woman carried her away" (790).

Later, the ring is found and brought to Dusyanta, causing him to remember his love for Śakuntala. Realizing his own loss, he pines for her, banning the festival of spring, neglecting his kingly duties, and gazing at a painting he made of her. At this point, he resembles Odysseus in that he suffers to redeem the separation from his wife and son. He says:

> I'm defenseless when I remember the pain of my love's bewilderment
> when I rejected her.
> When I cast her away, she followed her kinsmen,
> But Kanva's disciple harshly shouted, "Stay!"
> The tearful look my cruelty provoked
> Burns me like an arrow tipped with poison. (795)

A supernatural friend of Śakuntala overhears Dusyanta's lament and sees his suffering and reports that "Such words reveal that suffering has increased his modesty as much as his love" (797). Later, this friend says, "You have clearly atoned for the suffering your rejection caused Śakuntala" (798).

This statement reveals an awareness that suffering can redeem loss. Like Odysseus, Dusyanta does not die to redeem his lost family, but his suffering is the necessary catalyst to bring about that redemption. Shortly afterward, Dusyanta is called to lead the armies of the god Indra into battle against an army of demons. Although the battle is not reported directly, it functions much like Odysseus's journey into Hades as a symbolic death from which he can move on into his restored life. When he is returning in victory from his battle in the heavens, Dusyanta stops at the heavenly hermitage of another supernatural sage, which happens to be the place where Śakuntala and her young son have been in seclusion since Dusyanta's rejection of her. After some confusion, several supernatural signs lead to mutual recognitions, and the sage reports:

> By the turn of fortune,
> virtuous Śakuntala, her noble son,
> and the king are reunited—
> faith and wealth with order. (810)

In the end, the losses are restored. Although no innocent redeemer died, the sufferings of Śakuntala and Dusyanta have reestablished their love. The play ends with another brief hymn to Śiva, the creator, indicating that the cycle is complete and creation is redeemed.

⌒

Although none of these stories presents a perfect example of the pattern of redemption, each one demonstrates suffering that redeems loss. In Shakespeare's work, it seems that the redemptive pattern in *Hamlet* makes it a superior play to *Coriolanus*. Among the ancient Greeks, both Sophocles and Homer repeatedly present noble characters who are saved or who save others through suffering. And even in Hindu India, Kalidasa's *Śakuntala* follows the same scheme. It can be argued that these examples simply demonstrate the constraints of plot development—that any story requires complication and resolution. However, in the next chapter, a survey of the best-selling novels of all time will provide evidence that what makes a work successful is its deliberate use of the pattern of redemption.

# 3

## Redemption and Popularity

I F IT is true that the elements of creation, fall, and redemption make the ultimate archetypes underlying all narrative literature, then both enduring classics and popular literature should use these patterns in significant ways. Just as *Hamlet* seems to use them more effectively than *Coriolanus*, both "great" and popular works should reveal deeper kinds of redemption than minor works. There may of course be other factors causing popularity, such as extraliterary quirks of history or methods of publishing and advertising books, but other factors being equal, the Christian critic expects to find that the most popular works are the most redemptive works. If the ultimate human desire is for redemption from death, then people should inevitably be drawn to stories that present redemption.

Popularity can be difficult to measure. However, if data given by *Wikipedia* can be trusted, the most popular books of all time include the Bible and the writings of Mao Zedong, with more than five billion copies each.[1] The Bible is popular for both its value to the people of the largest religious group on earth and its obvious redemptive theme. The writings of Chairman Mao are probably popular because of governmental propagation within the largest nation on earth. Other religious books such as the *Koran* and the *Book of Mormon* and textbooks such as a Chinese dictionary and the *Boy Scout Handbook* have also sold more than 100 million

1. Wikipedia, "List of Best-Selling Books."

copies. However, focusing on more purely literary works, the best sellers of all time seem to be Charles Dickens' *A Tale of Two Cities*, with a claim of as many as 200 million copies; J. R. R. Tolkien's *The Lord of the Rings*, with 150 million; Agatha Christie's *And Then There Were None*, Tolkien's *The Hobbit*, and Cao Xueqin's *Dream of the Red Chamber*, with about 100 million each; and Antoine de Saint-Exupéry's *Le Petit Prince*, with about 80 million.[2]

## A TALE OF TWO CITIES

*A Tale of Two Cities* beautifully illustrates the principles of redemption criticism: it creates a fallen world, and it is built on the pattern of redemption. The story is set in a real time and place: the "two cities" of London and Paris during the revolutionary period from 1775 to 1792, facilitating the reader's belief in its reality. Paris, with its suburb of Saint Antoine in particular, is portrayed as a place of desolate poverty and oppression, desperately in need of redemption. The selfishness and cruelty of the ruling class, typified by the Marquis St. Evrémonde, has so impoverished and dehumanized the sans-culotterie that their representatives, Ernest and Thérèse Defarge, can think only of revenge. Madame Defarge tells her husband, "Vengeance and retribution require a long time; it is the rule."[3] Vengeance, like redemption, attempts to make right what is wrong. Like Christian redemption, it may require the shedding of blood. After a cask of wine is broken on the streets of Saint Antoine, one of the poor people who try to gather it up uses the wine to write the word "BLOOD" on a wall. The narrator then adds, "The time was to come, when that wine too would be spilled on the street-stones, and when the stain of it would be red upon many there" (33). But vengeance is a false redemption because it rights the wrong by punishment of the wrongdoer instead of by atonement for the wrong, naturally creating an ongoing cycle of wrongdoing.

2. These sales figures may not be reliable, especially in regards to *A Tale of Two Cities*, but each of these books has certainly been very popular.

3. Dickens, *A Tale of Two Cities*, 168.

Although the Defarges pursue this false redemption, every other major character in the novel performs some form of redemptive act. The otherwise crass Mr. Stryver provides legal redemption as defense counsel for Charles Darnay, getting him acquitted (with the help of Sydney Carton) of a capital charge of treason. The odd-job-man Jerry Cruncher portrays a parodic redemption of the dead in his moonlighting: taking bodies of the dead out of their graves to be used by physicians. The banker Jarvis Lorry provides physical redemptions, first delivering the young orphan Lucie Manette to safety in England and then delivering Doctor Alexandre Manette from prison and poverty in France. Charles Darnay attempts to redeem the wrongs done by his family when he renounces his heritage as the Marquis St. Evrémonde and remits the taxes of the peasants. He brings the plot to its crisis when he returns to Paris to try to redeem his family's former servant, Gabelle, imprisoned and threatened with execution by the Revolutionary Tribunal. Lucie Manette redeems her father (and, to a lesser extent, her husband) from the dementia caused by imprisonment through her faithful love.

In an article on Lucie's role as the traditional Victorian "angel in the house," Lisa Robson says: "In *A Tale of Two Cities* Dickens moves beyond the specifically traditional metaphor to highlight the angel's supposedly innate *redemptive* and regenerative abilities, her capacity to function as a type of *savior* figure. . . . While the angel figure as reflected in the women in the novel adheres to convention in its insistence on the female as the gentler, purer sex, it also emphasizes women's vital role as men's *redeemers*."[4] Lucie does not physically suffer to provide redemption, but she does submit her own life, in love, to the needs of her father (and husband) to bring a kind of salvation.

Two characters do actually use suffering to bring redemption. The first is Doctor Alexandre Manette. Dr. Manette had been "for eighteen years a secret and unaccused prisoner in the

4. Robson, "The 'Angels' in Dickens's House," 28; emphasis mine.

Bastille."[5] When released, he suffers dementia. Finally healed through his daughter Lucie's redemptive love, he remains a mostly passive figure in the novel until Lucie's husband, Charles Darnay, is captured in Paris and imprisoned as an illegal émigré by the Revolutionary Tribunal. At this point, Dr. Manette's status as a former prisoner under the old regime and as a physician working among the revolutionaries gives him a powerful voice in securing his son-in-law's freedom:

> For the first time the Doctor felt, now, that his suffering was strength and power. For the first time he felt that in that sharp fire, he had slowly forged the iron which could break the prison door of his daughter's husband and deliver him. "It all tended to a good end . . . ; it was not mere waste and ruin. As my beloved child was helpful in restoring me to myself, I will be helpful now in restoring the dearest part of herself to her; by the aid of Heaven I will do it!" (255–56)

When Charles is released, Dr. Manette proclaims, "I have saved him" (271). This salvation, however, is only temporary, as the Defarges bring new charges against Charles' family, supported by a letter Dr. Manette himself had written during his own imprisonment.

Finally then, the ultimate redeemer in *A Tale* is the dissipated and self-abnegating Sydney Carton. Carton saves Charles Darnay early in the novel by revealing to the court that is trying Darnay for treason how similar he and Darnay are in appearance. Then, in the final scene of the novel, Carton uses that similarity to substitute himself for Darnay and go to the guillotine in his place: a veritable substitutionary atonement. Here Carton utters one of the most famous lines in literature: "It is a far, far better thing that I do, than I have ever done; it is a far, far better rest that I go to than I have ever known" (351). As J. M. Rignall states, "It is not surprising that the most remembered scene in *A Tale of Two Cities* is the last, for this novel is dominated, even haunted, by its ending."[6] Rignall

---

5. Dickens, *A Tale of Two Cities*, 254.

6. Rignall, "Dickens and the Catastrophic Continuum of History," 13.

further claims that "for Dickens it is the Christ-like intervention of a self-sacrificing individual that is the vehicle for a vision of a better world which seems to lie beyond time and history."[7] On a narrative level, it seems strange that Carton should be perceived as such an essential figure since he plays seemingly minor roles in the plot before its melodramatic conclusion.

There are, however, at least three reasons why Carton's redemptive sacrifice is the most important act in the novel. First, although Carton is a relatively minor character until the final chapters, he is one of the few developing characters in the novel. Aside from Dr. Manette's transformations from demented prisoner to contented father to powerful agent for healing and redemption with the Revolutionary Tribunal, no other character experiences such profound change. Carton is a hopeless profligate living as the lawyer's "jackal" for Mr. Stryver until he begins to see good in himself, drawn out by his concealed love for Lucie Manette. Once he determines upon his self-sacrificial course, he not only stops drinking and remembers his promising youth but is able to reach out to give loving comfort to others, exemplified by the young seamstress who goes with him to the guillotine.[8]

Second, Carton's sacrifice resolves the novel's plot. The protagonist of the novel is not a single character, but the Manette/Darnay family. It is Dr. Manette, his daughter and son-in-law, and his granddaughter who are nearly lost and ultimately saved through the course of the plot. Carton not only saves them, but by loving Lucie and her daughter and substituting himself for Charles, he becomes a figurative member of this protagonist family. He is therefore central to the novel's structure.

Third, his sacrifice fits with the theme of resurrection that runs throughout the story. After the introductory chapter on "The Period," the first chapter of the plot climaxes with the utterance of the enigmatic code phrase "RECALLED TO LIFE" (16). This

7. Ibid., 14.

8. Dickens, *A Tale of Two Cities*, 331–32, 349–50.

code alludes to the figurative resurrection of Dr. Manette after his eighteen years of limbo in the Bastille. Following this is the emotional and intellectual resurrection of Dr. Manette brought about by Lucie's loving care. Later, both the French aristocrat Foulon and the British spy Roger Cly are "resurrected" after fake funerals, the latter of which is discovered as a result of Jerry Cruncher's business of stealing (and thereby "resurrecting") corpses (285). The young French aristocrat Saint Evrémonde is self-resurrected (or at least reinvented) as the hard-working Englishman Charles Darnay. Ultimately, as Carton contemplates his self-sacrificial death, he repeatedly remembers the words of Jesus: "I am the resurrection and the life, saith the Lord; he that believeth in me, though he were dead, yet shall he live: and whosoever liveth and believeth in me, shall never die."[9] Dickens deliberately ties Carton's death to the death and resurrection of Jesus.

Thus, Dickens has formed the narrative to focus the readers' attention on this one climactic action. This ostensibly most popular of all novels is unquestionably and in multiple ways a novel of redemption.

## THE LORD OF THE RINGS

Like *A Tale of Two Cities*, the second best-selling novel of all time is also dominated by the theme of redemption. J. R. R. Tolkien's fantasy epic *The Lord of the Rings* has apparently sold more than 150 million copies. It is surprising that such a long book—more than 1,100 pages, usually sold as a trilogy—should be so popular. Undoubtedly, the movies made of the book have boosted sales, yet it was popular long before Peter Jackson's successful films were released. Because Tolkien was an avowedly Christian writer, it is not surprising that *The Lord of the Rings* illustrates the pattern of redemption in ways that closely parallel Christian redemption. But it may not be a coincidence that the two best-selling novels of all time are both dominated by the theme of redemption.

9. John 11:25–26; ibid., 294, 295, 350.

Looking at the three parts of the redemptive pattern, it can be said first of all that *The Lord of the Rings* is a novel of creation *par excellence*. Tolkien's Middle Earth is created practically *ex nihilo* in such detail that it can even make claims by alluding to tangential stories in its own prehistory, such as the story of the elf-maiden Lúthien Tinúviel and her human lover Beren.[10] And although it is a world with creatures, cultures, and powers foreign to the real world, most readers seem to have little difficulty suspending their disbelief and entering into the lives of its elves, orcs, wizards, dwarves, Rohirrim, and hobbits.

Secondly, Middle Earth is clearly a fallen world. The golden age of the Kings of Númenor is long past, and the rise of the evil lord Sauron threatens to destroy all the goodness that remains. Not only the distant past but also the realms of Rivendell, Lórien, and even the Shire all represent Edenic places, each of which is threatened with destruction.

Most importantly, all throughout the novel one character after another dies or approaches death to save others. Gandalf, Boromir, the Ents, Aragorn, Faramir, Théoden, Éowyn, Pippin, Merry, and Frodo all willingly risk or give their lives to save others. Gandalf goes first and establishes the redemptive pattern. As the fellowship of the ring is chased through the Mines of Moria by the evil and powerful Balrog, Gandalf orders the others, "Fly! This is a foe beyond any of you. I must hold the narrow way. Fly!"[11] After he falls into an abyss with the Balrog, it is reported, "Gandalf was our guide, and he led us through Moria; and when our escape seemed beyond hope he saved us, and he fell."[12] Not only is Gandalf a good and great savior, but he approaches Christlikeness when he is later resurrected: "Behold, I am not Gandolf the Grey, whom you betrayed. I am Gandalf the White, who has returned from death."[13]

---

10. Tolkien, *The Return of the King*, 157, 273.

11. Tolkien, *The Fellowship of the Ring*, 321.

12. Ibid., 346.

13. Tolkien, *The Two Towers*, 208.

Later, Boromir falls to the temptation to try to seize the Ring, but he redeems himself by giving his own life in battle trying to save the hobbits. The Ents risk annihilation when they attack the evil wizard Saruman. Treebeard says, "Of course, it is likely enough . . . that we are going to our doom: the last march of the Ents. . . . Now at least the last march of the Ents may be worth a song. . . . we may help the other peoples before we pass away."[14] Aragorn must seek "the Paths of the Dead,"[15] risking his own life to raise an army that can save the city of Minas Tirith. Faramir is nearly killed, and Théoden is killed, fighting to save Minas Tirith. Éowyn and Merry both approach death after their struggle against the evil Lord of the Nazgûl. Pippin is all but killed in the last battle, at the Black Gate: "Blackness and stench and crushing pain came upon Pippin, and his mind fell away into a great darkness. . . . And his thought fled far away and his eyes saw no more."[16]

Ultimately, the novel is about Frodo, the Ringbearer, who must save all of Middle Earth by destroying the Ring of Power. Frodo experiences various near deaths, risking his life to the very end. Early in the novel, Frodo learns that he must undertake a "perilous quest," and Gandalf tells him, "you have been chosen."[17] Frodo responds, "I should like to save the Shire, if I could."[18] So it is established that Frodo is chosen by a greater power and that he is given a role as a savior. His first encounter with death also comes early in the novel, after he is stabbed with a cursed knife by one of the Ringwraiths and slowly succumbs to its power: "Then Frodo felt himself falling, and the roaring and confusion seemed to rise and engulf him together with his enemies. He saw and heard no more."[19] This wound is healed by elves, though Frodo feels it until

14. Ibid., 92.
15. Tolkien, *The Return of the King*, 45.
16. Ibid., 176–77.
17. Tolkien, *The Fellowship of the Ring*, 60.
18. Ibid., 61.
19. Ibid., 209.

the end of the story. Later, in the Mines of Moria, Frodo is again close to death when he is stabbed by a cave troll, although this time he is saved by his hidden armor.

After a council is held to determine what to do with the Ring, Frodo's calling is confirmed. "The Council laid it upon me to bear it," he says.[20] He soon realizes that he must bear his burden alone: " 'I will do now what I must,' he said. 'This at least is plain: the evil of the Ring is already at work even in the Company, and the Ring must leave them before it does more harm. I will go alone.' "[21] Such statements seem to be if not allegory, at least a deliberate ploy by Tolkien to make readers think of Christ bearing the cross alone for the salvation of others. Much of the last third of the novel can be seen as Frodo's *via dolorosa*, bearing his burden through the terrible landscapes of Minas Morgul, Shelob's lair, and the plains of Mordor, leading to "Mount Doom."

Frodo suffers another near death when he is bitten by the evil giant spider Shelob. When his companion Sam finds him lifeless and wrapped in her web, he says, "Don't leave me here alone! . . . Don't go where I can't follow!"[22] This again may be a deliberate allusion to Jesus Christ, who says to Peter shortly before the crucifixion, "Where I am going you cannot follow Me now" (John 13:36). Frodo recovers yet again and proceeds onward to Mount Doom. Reaching there after a terrible struggle, he finally says, "Farewell, Sam! This is the end at last. On Mount Doom doom shall fall. Farewell."[23] Once the Ring is destroyed, Mount Doom itself erupts all around Frodo, and he says, "the Quest is achieved, and now all is over."[24] Yet even here Frodo is rescued by Gandalf and the great eagles, so in the end Frodo does fall short of giving his life to bring redemption to Middle Earth. Nevertheless, at the

20. Ibid., 390.
21. Ibid., 392.
22. Tolkien, *The Two Towers*, 384.
23. Ibid., 237.
24. Ibid., 241.

close of the novel, Frodo neatly summarizes the theme of redemption: "I tried to save the Shire, and it has been saved, but not for me. It must often be so, Sam, when things are in danger: some one has to give them up, lose them, so that others may keep them."[25] Frodo has suffered so much to save all that he loves that he can no longer enjoy his old life, and he sails away from the Grey Havens "and passed on into the West."[26]

## THE DREAM OF THE RED CHAMBER

Cao Xuequin's eighteenth-century novel of manners, *The Dream of the Red Chamber*, is difficult to evaluate for several reasons. One is that, as with the writings of Chairman Mao Zedong, its popularity may result simply from being written in the language of the most populous nation on earth. Another is that the upper-class Chinese culture portrayed in the novel is so different from my own that I can't always be sure of the implications of the characters' words and actions. Probably the biggest difficulty comes from the disputed provenance of the novel, which seems to have been started by one author and finished by another, with critics debating the value of the long conclusion added by the second author. According to Jeanne Knoerle, "Critics tend to think that the last forty chapters are of markedly poor literary quality, which they suspect proves that Kao E completed the novel on his own inspiration, giving it, for example, a happier ending than was originally intended by his allowing Pao-yü to pass the Imperial Examinations."[27]

With all that said, one can still say that the novel vividly creates the world of the noble Chinese household of the Yungkuofu, where most of the story occurs, and that this household and several key members of it experience economic or spiritual failures that constitute falls. Most importantly, however, the novel, at least in C.

25. Tolkien, *The Return of the King*, 338.
26. Ibid., 339.
27. Knoerle, *The Dream of the Red Chamber*, 5–6.

C. Wang's condensed translation, does seem to be built upon two essential kinds of redemption. One is a kind of spiritual redemption. The novel begins in a realm outside of time and space (outside "the red dust"). Here, two heavenly beings—a Taoist monk and a Buddhist monk—meet and agree to descend to "the mortal world": " 'I propose,' the Taoist said, 'that we go down to the mortal world ourselves when the time comes and save a few that are especially worth saving.' "[28] At the end, the novel returns to this "heavenly" realm. Knoerle explains:

> The translator's selection process, too, alters the aesthetic pattern of time and space in the story. C. C. Wang makes of the book, despite its 564-page length, a clear story of the people who reside in the Chia mansions. . . . He retains almost all of the supernatural and philosophical material that opens the book but suppresses a good deal of the material at the end, making the preincarnation-incarnation-postincarnation story complete, but somewhat out of proportion, and making Pao-yü's final actions somewhat precipitate and philosophically unprepared for."[29]

Therefore, although I cannot claim to have a thorough understanding of the implications of these supernatural events, it seems likely that this pattern of "preincarnation-incarnation-postincarnation" fits the pattern of fall and redemption that has characterized the other works discussed so far.

The second kind of redemption in the novel is that of the Chia family. Once wealthy and powerful, the family suffers as one member is accused of corruption, another, Wang Hsi-fang (Phoenix), falls from favor, and the entire household declines in wealth and honor. Meanwhile, the protagonist, Pao-yü, is a sort of rebel, resisting his father's authority and preferring poetry and the company of young women over his studies and his family's honor. Ultimately, however, Pao-yü seems to set aside his own desires

---

28. Tsao Hsueh-chin, *Dream of the Red Chamber*, 6–7.

29. Knoerle, *The Dream of the Red Chamber*, 115.

for the good of the family and unexpectedly scores high on his Imperial Examinations, redeeming his and his family's honor.

At the end, Pao-yü—who seems to have been an incarnation of a spiritual entity all along—renounces "the red dust" (the material world) and returns to the spiritual realm from which he came. Knoerle says, "By rejecting the Red Dust and its responsibilities, Pao-yü is the only character in the novel who undergoes a moral conversion and thereby attains immortality."[30] Although he is not otherwise a Christlike character, his human incarnation and final return to a heavenly realm create an obvious parallel with the Christian pattern. In summary, therefore, despite the literary and cultural complexities of this novel, it does appear to support my claim that the most popular works of literature are built on the pattern of redemption.

## *LE PETIT PRINCE*

Although Antoine de Saint-Exupéry's *Le Petit Prince* is not a major novel in the same sense as *A Tale of Two Cities*, *The Lord of the Rings*, or *The Dream of the Red Chamber*, it is a fictional narrative, and it may have sold as many as 80 million copies worldwide. Like Tolkien's works, its creativity is based not on the world as we know it but on the creation of its own universe, a universe of planets (or asteroids) inhabited by individuals: a king, a vain man, a drunkard, a businessman, a lighter of streetlamps, a geographer, the little prince himself, and on earth, a serpent, a fox, a switchman, and a pilot/narrator. Each planet is absurd—the earth most of all—but each incarnates a satirical or poignant reality strongly linked to the world we experience daily. The narrator's frequent appeals to children, as opposed to *"les grandes personnes,"* also play upon a childlike willingness to suspend disbelief.

What is most striking about *Le Petit Prince* is that although it is ostensibly a children's book, its climax is the sacrificial death

30. Ibid., 78.

of the hero. The narrator, lost in the Sahara after the breakdown of his airplane engine, encounters a little prince who has traveled through the solar system seeking a way to save his world from baobab trees, which threaten to crush the tiny asteroid, while at the same time protecting his beloved flower. The prince has met a number of absurd "*grandes personnes*" on his travels, but he comments that only one did not seem ridiculous, a man who spent all his time lighting and extinguishing the only streetlamp on his tiny asteroid because "*c'est la consign*": "That's the orders."[31] The little prince remarks: "*c'est le seul qui ne me paraisse pas ridicule. C'est, peut-être, parce qu'il s'occupe d'autre chose que de soi-même*" ("this is the only one who does not seem ridiculous to me. Maybe that's because he takes care of something other than himself").[32] Here, the prince himself recognizes the value of sacrificial giving, of living for "something other than himself."

The little prince also recognizes the fact of death. He is horrified when he realizes "*Ma fleur est menacé de disparition prochaine? . . . Ma fleur est éphémère!*" (My flower is threatened by imminent disappearance? . . . My flower is ephemeral!" [39]).The narrator draws/incarnates for the prince a sheep, which can graze on the baobab shoots, and a muzzle for the sheep to prevent it from eating the flower (which has only four thorns to protect itself). However, the narrator is himself "*éphémère*," lost in the desert, struggling to repair his airplane, and running out of water.

The little prince saves the narrator, leading him through the trackless desert to a well of water. He knows of this well because it is near the place where he first came to earth. It is also at this place that he first met the serpent. The serpent had told him, "*Celui que je touche, je le rends à la terre dont il est sorti*" ("Whomever I touch, I return him to the earth from which he came" [41]). Clearly, this is a biblical allusion (see Genesis 3:19), so it is all the more significant that the serpent adds, "*Mais tu es pur et tu viens d'une étoile*"

31. Saint-Exupéry, *Le Petit Prince*, 35.

32. Ibid., 36; translation mine throughout.

("But you are pure and you come from a star" [41]). Thus, the little prince is both human and heavenly; he is pure of sin; and his death will return him not to earth but to the heavens. When he meets a garden full of roses, he tells them, "*Vous êtes belles, mais vous êtes vides. . . . On ne peut pas mourir pour vous*" ("You all are beautiful, but you are empty. . . . One can't die for you" [47]). Hence, he recognizes the possibility of dying for another and implies that he will die for his own flower. At the end, he meets with the serpent to receive a fatal bite. In the morning, the narrator cannot find his body and implies that he must have ascended back to his asteroid. Thus the Little Prince has become the savior/redeemer of both the narrator and his own little planet.

## HARRY POTTER AND THE DEATHLY HALLOWS

A recent best seller that clearly relies on the death of the redeemer is the young adult series of Harry Potter books. Looking just at the last in the seven-book series, *Wikipedia* reports that sales of *Harry Potter and the Deathly Hallows* have been record-setting. "On opening day, a record 8.3 million copies were sold in the United States, and 2.65 million copies in the United Kingdom. At WH Smith, sales reportedly reached a rate of 15 books sold per second. By June 2008, nearly a year after it was published, worldwide sales were reportedly around 44 million."[33] Throughout this record-selling book, Harry Potter repeatedly recalls the people who have given their lives to protect him, including his parents, his godfather Sirius Black, and his mentor Albus Dumbledore. Then, at a key moment in the plot, another friend, the elf named Dobby, dies rescuing him. In the climactic battle between Harry's friends and the forces of the evil Voldemort, several more of his friends are killed before Voldemort accuses Harry: "You have permitted your friends to die for you rather than face me yourself."[34] Harry feels

33. Wikipedia, "Harry Potter and the Deathly Hallows."
34. Rowling, *Harry Potter and the Deathly Hallows*, 660.

that he can no longer accept such sacrifices—"He could not bear . . . to see who else had died for him"(662)—and he determines to face Voldemort. While on his way to face him, he learns that Voldemort can be destroyed only if he kills Harry.

At this moment, Harry Potter becomes the innocent redeemer. He decides that he "would not let anyone else die for him now that he had discovered it was in his power to stop it. . . . Like rain on a cold window, these thoughts pattered against the hard surface of the incontrovertible truth, which was that he must die. I must die. It must end" (693). This is not only a Heideggerian realization that he must face death "authentically," but also an understanding that he can offer his life to save others. His self-sacrifice will save the lives of his friends and bring an end to the evil that is threatening to seize control of his world. So Harry approaches Voldemort and allows himself to be killed.

However, in a further parallel with the Christian pattern of redemption, Harry does not remain dead. Because his own life is supernaturally tied to Voldemort's, he returns from death to the world and faces Voldemort once again.

> "You won't be killing anyone else tonight," said Harry as they circled, and stared into each other's eyes, green into red. "You won't be able to kill any of them ever again. Don't you get it? I was ready to die to stop you from hurting these people—"
> "But you did not!"
> "—I meant to, and that's what did it." (738)

Voldemort tries to kill Harry again but dies as his own killing curse rebounds on him, unable to harm the innocent redeemer who has already given his life for others.

One may argue that the Harry Potter books have been phenomenally popular because, much like Tolkien's *Lord of the Rings*, they create an appealing, magical world. Furthermore, their simple prose and adolescent hero make them appealing to the children and young adults who have been their main audience. And unquestionably, as with *Lord of the Rings* and *Gone with the Wind*, movie versions have boosted sales of the books. Nevertheless, they provide yet one more piece of evidence that a key factor—maybe the key factor—that makes stories appeal to audiences is the pattern of loss redeemed by the innocent redeemer. The pattern among these best-selling novels should be clear by now. Looking at *A Tale of Two Cities*, *The Lord of the Rings*, *The Dream of the Red Chamber*, *The Little Prince*, and *Harry Potter and the Deathly Hallows*, we find that each not merely includes but is built on a structure of sacrificial death to bring redemption.

Focusing next on American best sellers, relatively precise figures on popularity before 1950 can be found in Frank Luther Mott's classic study of popular literature in America, *Golden Multitudes: The Story of Best Sellers in the United States*. Mott establishes the arbitrary criterion that to be a best seller, a book must have total sales equaling at least one percent of the U.S. population for the decade in which it was first published in America. Omitting "bibles, hymnals, textbooks, almanacs, cookbooks, doctor-books, manuals, and reference works," he found 324 best sellers from Michael Wigglesworth's 1662 *The Day of Doom* to Kathleen Winsor's 1945 *Forever Amber*.[35] Ideally, a comparison of a sample of these 324 books with an equal number of poor sellers might show what makes a book popular, at least in America before 1950. However, as Mott points out:

> There are too many impalpable considerations, too many chances and accidents, too complex a combination of conditions affecting the writing, publication, and selling of a book to make the attainment of the top rank by even the most promising candidate a certainty. The creation of a best seller does not follow an exact pattern, or patterns, any more than does the making of a successful man; there are too many intangibles, too many unmeasurable human values, too many vicissitudes of fortune involved.[36]

35. Mott, *Golden Multitudes*, 303–15.
36. Ibid., 285.

The very fact that some of the best sellers of all time are not even narratives—textbooks, dictionaries, etc.—proves that there are other considerations besides the pattern of redemptive action that determine the sales appeal of a book. Yet, as Mott explores possible factors in popularity, the first he considers is "religious appeal," which he says "is strong from one end of the list to the other."[37] This could obviously tie in with Christian redemption, whether it is transparent, as in *The Day of Doom*, *Pilgrim's Progress*, and Lloyd Douglas's 1942 *The Robe*, or more figurative, as in Steinbeck's *The Grapes of Wrath*. Other factors that Mott considers, such as "self-improvement," historicity, and "vividness," could well tie in with the cycle of creation, fall, and redemption.

Mott found seven works that had sold more than 2.5 million copies: Shakespeare's *Plays*, *Mother Goose*, *Gone with the Wind*, *Uncle Tom's Cabin*, *How to Win Friends and Influence People*, *Ivanhoe*, and *Ben-Hur*.[38] After the Bible and various nonfiction books, these were the all-time best sellers in America before 1950. This is a diverse set of works, but if they each reveal significant uses of the pattern of redemption, this will provide evidence for my theory of Christian criticism. Shakespeare's *Plays* and *Mother Goose* are collections, of which the individual works need to be analyzed separately elsewhere, and *How to Win Friends and Influence People* is also from a different genre that would need to be analyzed in a different way. But looking at the four novels, one notices immediately that they are all either historical novels or topical novels. This suggests that they deliberately try to create in fictional form the world as people know it. Americans have long preferred historical fiction over more imaginative forms, perhaps because, as a relatively young nation, they desire to create a sense of their own historicity or perhaps as a way to assuage the Puritan heritage of distrust for the "falsehood" of fiction. Both of these causes connect to the notion that good literature is creative—it attempts to recreate the real world. But beyond

37. Ibid., 286.
38. Ibid., 261.

this very basic claim, I would also assert that all four of these best sellers are built on the pattern of loss and redemption that is central to all good literature.

## *IVANHOE*

Sir Walter Scott's 1820 *Ivanhoe* is the only foreign novel among Mott's top seven books. Though clearly a romantic novel, its setting in twelfth-century England creates a realistic-enough world, at least for the relatively unsophisticated reading audience in nineteenth-century America. The world Scott creates is believable because of historical characters, such as King Richard the Lion-Heart and Prince John; well-known cultural features, such as the conflict of Anglo-Saxons against Normans and the Knights Templar against the civil order; and extensive footnotes on such details as negroes in medieval England,[39] the torture of laymen invested with ecclesiastical revenues,[40] and the architecture of Saxon fortifications.[41]

The plot of *Ivanhoe* involves several interrelated stories of fall and redemption. For example, the Saxons have lost their kingdom to the Normans, and Cedric the Saxon strives to restore the Anglo-Saxon monarchy. When captured by Normans, Cedric expresses his willingness to die as a Saxon redeemer: "Put us, then, to death, and complete your tyranny by taking our lives, as you began with our liberties. If the Saxon Cedric cannot rescue England, he is willing to die for her" (223). At the same time, England is in danger of falling from the rule of the good King Richard into the hands of his scheming and cruel brother Prince John. Both of these falls are resolved when Richard returns to England, reclaims his throne, and gives the Saxons a "prospect of attaining their just rights" (496). The separation of the lovers Rowena and Ivanhoe follows a comic redemption pattern. Difficulties are overcome:

39. Scott, *Ivanhoe*, 42.
40. Ibid., 233–40.
41. Ibid., 458–63.

Rowena is rescued from kidnappers; Ivanhoe's rival Athelstane renounces his claims; Richard makes Ivanhoe's father Cedric drop his opposition. But no redeemer offers his life.

Next, the Jews in the story, Isaac of York and his daughter Rebecca, live in a fallen world where they are subject to ridicule, bigotry, oppression, and extortion on every side. Rebecca is willing to die as a redeemer of her people: "Would to heaven that the shedding of my own blood, drop by drop, could redeem the captivity of Judah!" (317). In the end, however, they have only an ongoing search for a place of safety. Rebecca says: "My father hath a brother in high favor with Mohammed Boabdil, King of Grenada—thither we go, secure of peace and protection, for the payment of such ransom as the Moslems exact from our people (497).This "redemption" will be paid for literally, with gold.

None of these stories includes a Christlike redeemer, offering his or her life to save those who are lost, and if there were no more to the novel, its popularity would seem to counter my argument for the necessity of the redeemer in literature. However, the ultimate and climactic conflict in the novel entails the capture, attempted seduction, and deliverance of Rebecca. Brian de Bois-Guilbert is a powerful but atheistic and amoral Templar knight. He becomes obsessed with Rebecca's beauty and, after taking her prisoner, repeatedly attempts to seduce her. She resists, but when the Grand Master of the Templars learns that one of his best "Christian" knights is holding an "infidel" Jewish woman, he assumes that she must have bewitched him and condemns her to burn at the stake. She appeals for a champion to deliver her in trial by combat against Bois-Guilbert. At the novel's climax, Ivanhoe arrives as her champion just in time on an exhausted horse and still recovering from a serious wound he had received a few days earlier:

> The wearied horse of Ivanhoe, and its no less exhausted rider, went down, as all had expected, before the well-aimed lance and vigorous steed of the Templar. This issue of the combat all had foreseen; but although the spear of Ivanhoe did but, in comparison, touch the shield of Bois-Guilbert, that champion, to the astonishment of all who beheld it, reeled in his saddle, lost his stirrups, and fell in the lists. . . . Unscathed by the lance of his enemy, he had died a victim to the violence of his own contending passions.
>
> "This is indeed the judgment of God," said the Grand Master, looking upwards—"*Fiat voluntas tua!*" (488)

Although Ivanhoe does not die to save Rebecca, he fits many criteria of a true redeemer. Throughout the story, he is honest, noble, courageous, self-sacrificing, and kind: a good man. He feels gratitude to Rebecca for her treatment of his wound, but he has nothing to gain for himself when he goes to rescue her, so he is risking his life for another. He had been wounded by a spear in his side: probably an intentional parallel to Jesus, who was pierced on the cross (John 19:34). Although he does not die, he is defeated by his evil enemy and apparently would have been killed had not Bois-Guilbert been killed by "the judgment of God." Thus Ivanhoe, one of the most popular novels of its century, is a novel of redemption.

## BEN-HUR: A TALE OF THE CHRIST

Lew Wallace's *Ben-Hur: A Tale of the Christ* is almost too transparently redemptive to need explanation. In the second chapter, young Judah Ben-Hur accidentally injures the Roman procurator Gratus, leading to the imprisonment of his mother and sister and his own condemnation as a galley slave. The rest of the book is the story of Ben-Hur's quest for various kinds of redemption. He achieves personal redemption from slavery when he risks his own life to save the Roman admiral Quintus Arrius. He is redeemed from bitterness and shame in a chariot race when he defeats and cripples Messala, his former Roman friend who had betrayed him. He transcends an empty, materialistic Roman way of life when his former servant Simonides voluntarily submits to him. His mother and sister are redeemed from prison by the kindness of a Roman guard and are healed of leprosy by Jesus on Palm Sunday. And finally, Ben-Hur is spiritually redeemed, in the traditional Christian sense, after watching the crucifixion of Jesus and believing in Jesus as the Divine Redeemer. Wallace's redemptive theme is defined at the midpoint of the novel by Balthasar, one of the wise men who sought and found the baby Jesus at his birth:

> That which drove me at last into the solitude where the Spirit found me—was the fallen condition of men, occasioned, as I believed, by the loss of the knowledge of God. I sorrowed for the sorrows of my kind—not of one class, but all of them. So utterly were they fallen it seemed to me there could be no Redemption unless God himself would make it his work; and I prayed him to come, and that I might see him. "Thy good works have conquered. The Redemption cometh; thou shalt see the Saviour"—thus the Voice spake; and with the answer I went up to Jerusalem rejoicing. Now, to whom is the Redemption? To all the world. . . . The Redemption cannot be for a political purpose—to pull down rulers and powers, and vacate their places merely that others may take and enjoy them. . . . I tell you, though it be but the saying of blind to blind, he that comes is to be a Saviour of souls; and the Redemption means God once more on earth, and righteousness, that his stay here may be tolerable to himself.[42]

Obviously, Wallace was openly polemical in using this novel to teach a Christian doctrine of redemption. And it appears that this overt use of the theme of Christian redemption may have enhanced the popularity of the novel, which sold more than 2.6 million copies by 1950.

---

42. Wallace, *Ben-Hur*, 278–79.

## UNCLE TOM'S CABIN

The most popular American novel of the nineteenth century is Harriet Beecher Stowe's 1852 *Uncle Tom's Cabin*. Mott claims that "there have been few world successes to equal that of *Uncle Tom's Cabin* since its publication."[43] There is no doubt that the contemporary topicality of the work contributed to its popularity. And yet, with many novels written about topical issues, is it not significant that the particular topical issue of the best-selling American book of the nineteenth century is the abolition of slavery—a redemptive theme if there ever was one?

The creativity of *Uncle Tom's Cabin* is based, like that of any historical novel, on imitation of the real world. Yet few novels go so far to assert the accuracy of their imitation. Stowe asserts in her preface that "these representations" are based on "personal knowledge the author has had, of the truth of incidents such as here are related."[44] Just one year after the 1852 publication of the novel, she brought out *A Key to Uncle Tom's Cabin*, a major work documenting examples of the events and character types shown in the novel. Today many readers find the novel overly melodramatic and romanticized, but the author could not have claimed more strongly that she was creating a realistic picture of the actual world of slavery.

In this created world, the theme of redemption works on many levels, in almost every aspect of *Uncle Tom's Cabin*. On a sociohistorical level, there is the claim that this book was a factor in provoking the American Civil War, in which hundreds of thousands gave their lives to redeem the nation from slavery and division. Abraham Lincoln saw the war in redemptive terms, as he urged in his Gettysburg Address "that these dead shall not have died in vain—that this nation, under God, shall have a new birth of freedom." And there is the well-known report that Lincoln re-

---

43. Mott, *Golden Multitudes*, 119.
44. Stowe, *The Oxford Harriet Beecher Stowe Reader*, 81.

ferred to *Uncle Tom's Cabin* as "the book that made this big war."[45] Few novels indeed can make such a claim to have influenced a redemptive movement in history.

Within the novel itself, there is a variety of examples of both failed redemption and successful redemption. Failed redemption, for example, occurs when St. Clare dies suddenly just days before he was to free Tom, although St. Clare himself is probably redeemed in the purely Christian sense on his deathbed, largely through the influence of Tom, who earlier had said, "I's willing to lay down my life, this blessed day, to see Mas'r a Christian."[46] Another failed redemption is the haunting vignette of the slave woman Lucy, whom Tom meets on a riverboat going down to New Orleans. She despairs after her child is separated from her and sold:

> Tom drew near, and tried to say something; but she only groaned. Honestly, and with tears running down his cheeks, he spoke of a heart of love in the skies, of a pitying Jesus, and an eternal home; but the ear was deaf with anguish, and the palsied heart could not feel. . . .
>
> At midnight, Tom waked, with a sudden start. Something black passed quickly by him to the side of the boat, and he heard a splash in the water. No one else saw or heard anything. He raised his head,—the woman's place was vacant! (175)

This scene portrays pure desolation. The woman has suffered an unbearable loss, and Tom's comforting words are ineffectual. As a result of this failure of redemption, the woman is dehumanized— she becomes "something black"—and she passes into annihilation: "The poor bleeding heart was still, at last, and the river rippled and dimpled just as brightly as if it had not closed above it" (175).

Two more failed redemptions dominate the conclusion of the story. One is the arrival of George Shelby at the Legree plantation just hours too late to save Tom's life. The audience feels the bitterness of fate, the emptiness of what almost was. Yet the true horror

---

45. Quoted in McMichael, *Anthology of American Literature*, 1893.
46. Stowe, *Oxford Harriet Beecher Stowe Reader*, 299.

within *Uncle Tom's Cabin* is the anti-redemption of Simon Legree. Tom tries to offer him redemption:

> "Mas'r, if you was sick, or in trouble, or dying, and I could save ye, I'd *give* ye my heart's blood; and, if taking every drop of blood in this poor old body would save your precious soul, I'd give 'em freely, as the Lord gave his for me. O, Mas'r! don't bring this great sin on your soul! . . ."
>
> . . . Legree stood aghast, and looked at Tom; and there was such a silence, that the tick of the old clock could be heard, measuring, with silent touch, the last moments of mercy and probation to that hardened heart.
>
> It was but a moment. There was one hesitating pause,—one irresolute, relenting thrill,—and the spirit of evil came back, with seven-fold vehemence; and Legree, foaming with rage, smote his victim to the ground. (379–80)

Having hardened his heart against this proffer of redemption, Legree is now lost beyond reclamation. He dies in drunken, haunted misery. Stowe seems to have deliberately used this pattern of alternating scenes of redemption with such antiredemptions to increase the emotional intensity of the story.

Ultimately, *Uncle Tom's Cabin* is the story of two redeemers: Eva St. Clare and Uncle Tom. Both are portrayed as good, innocent, and loving, and both die while bringing redemption to others. Eva's death particularly brings both freedom from slavery and possible Christian salvation to the previously reprobate slave girl Topsy. Tom, although failing to redeem Lucy and Legree, offers himself for his family and the others on the Shelby plantation, for Augustine St. Clare, for Legree's slave women Cassy and Emmeline, and for the overseer slaves on Legree's plantation, Sambo and Quimbo. When the Shelbys must sell Tom or lose their plantation and all their slaves, Tom tells his wife, "If I must be sold, or all the people on the place, and everything go to rack, why, let me be sold. I s'pose I can b'ar it as well as any on 'em" (109). As Augustine St. Clare is dying of knife wounds, Tom tells him, "I's willin' to lay down my life, this blessed day, to see Mas'r a Christian" (299). When Legree threatens to kill Tom if he won't reveal the whereabouts of Cassy and Emmeline and demands, "Do you know anything?" Tom, who knows their hiding place and escape plans, says, "I know, Mas'r; but I can't tell anything. *I can die!*" (379). Finally, after Sambo and Quimbo have beaten Tom beyond recovery at Legree's orders, Tom says to them, "Poor critters . . . I'd be willing to bar' all I have, if it'll only bring ye to Christ! O, Lord! Give me these two more souls, I pray!" And the narrator reports, "That prayer was answered!" (381).

It is hardly surprising that Harriet Beecher Stowe, daughter of an evangelist and wife of a theology professor, would fill her novel with so many redemptive narratives. What is significant, however, is that this book, the most successful and influential American novel of its century, is from beginning to end and at every level a novel about redemption.

～

Looking at the most popular American novels of the twentieth century reveals a shift away from such purely redemptive stories. Russell Ash asserts in *The Top Ten of Everything, 2007* that Jacqueline Susann's *Valley of the Dolls* "is perhaps surprisingly the world's bestselling novel. Margaret Mitchell's *Gone with the Wind*, which has achieved sales approaching 28,000,000, is its closest rival."[47] What may be most significant about the structures of these novels is that both follow one of the most popular literary formulae of all time, what has sometimes been called the "woman's romance." This genre is typically based on the quest for a redeemer-husband. Austen's *Pride and Prejudice* and Brontë's *Jane Eyre* are classic examples. In this genre, a woman (usually young, beautiful, and intelligent) seeks a husband with the hope that he will save her from poverty, a shameful past, or just the menial lot of women.

47. Ash, *The Top Ten of Everything*, 113. Ash seems to have more conservative figures than *Wikipedia's* "List of Best-sellers." Book sales are notoriously hard to track.

Most often the pattern is comic, with the young woman finding and marrying her true love and rising above the pathetic life for which she had seemed to be destined. In the twentieth century, Williams' *The Glass Menagerie* presents a similar quest for what he calls the "gentleman caller," although in typical twentieth-century fashion, he presents an ironic and failed quest. Likewise playing almost satirically with the conventional pattern, both *Gone with the Wind* and *Valley of the Dolls* follow failed quests for redeemer husbands.

## GONE WITH THE WIND

Unlike earlier American classics such as *Uncle Tom's Cabin* and *Ben-Hur*, Mitchell's *Gone with the Wind* has little overtly Christian content and no obvious Christian themes. And yet, from beginning to end, it is about redemption. Scarlett O'Hara is a selfish and manipulative Southern belle. After war destroys the pampered, genteel life that she grew up with, she struggles for years to redeem her losses through her quests for money and for her idealized redeemer-lover, Ashley Wilkes. During a conversation with Ashley late in the novel, she asks herself:

> Where did she want to get? That was a silly question. Money and security, of course. And yet—Her mind fumbled. She had money and as much security as one could hope for in an insecure world. But, now that she thought about it, they weren't quite enough. Now that she thought about it, they hadn't made her particularly happy, though they had made her less harried, less fearful of the morrow. If I'd had money and security and you [Ashley], that would have been where I wanted to get, she thought, looking at him yearningly.[48]

However, at the end, when Ashley is finally free to marry her, she realizes that her ideal of him as her redeemer is false: "'He never really existed at all, except in my imagination,' she thought wearily. 'I loved something I made up. . . . I made a pretty suit

48. Mitchell, *Gone with the Wind*, 923.

of clothes and fell in love with it. And when Ashley came riding along, so handsome, so different, I put that suit on him and made him wear it whether it fitted him or not. And I wouldn't see what he really was. I kept on loving the pretty clothes—and not him at all'" (1016).

In fact, the story is full of false redeemers. Charles Hamilton marries Scarlett and dies in the war, leaving her as selfish and unfulfilled as she began. Scarlett's mother, Ellen, who had always guided her and provided the example of a kind and self-sacrificing "great lady," dies of typhus before Scarlett can return home to see her, but leaves only a void in Scarlett's life. Mammy continually tries to protect and guide Scarlett, finally giving up and abandoning her after Scarlett's child Bonnie dies. Frank Kennedy marries her (providing money for her literally to redeem her family plantation, Tara) and is killed while taking part in a Ku Klux Klan raid to defend Scarlett's honor. Yet Scarlett feels only guilt: "now he was dead because of her obstinacy. God would punish her for that" (821). "God" is mentioned several times in the novel, but typically as an empty religious concept. As the narrator says, "Religion had always been a bargaining process with Scarlett. She promised God good behavior in exchange for favors" (510).

Rhett Butler appears repeatedly throughout the story to rescue Scarlett: from widowhood after Charles' death, from the burning of Atlanta near the end of the war, finally marrying her after Frank's death and providing her with practically unlimited wealth and security. At the end, she does recognize Rhett as a redeemer: "It was Rhett—Rhett who had strong arms to hold her, a broad chest to pillow her tired head, jeering laughter to pull her affairs into proper perspective. And complete understanding, because he, like her, saw truth as truth, unobstructed by impractical notions of honor, sacrifice, or high belief in human nature. He loved her" (1021). But ultimately he, too, is a false redeemer, asking Scarlett, "did it ever occur to you that even the most deathless love could wear out?" and asserting, "Mine wore out. . . . Mine wore out" (1029).

There is, in the end, one true redeemer in the story: Melanie Hamilton Wilkes. Melanie is portrayed as completely selfless, loyal, and caring: "Because she had always been happy, she wanted everyone about her to be happy or, at least, pleased with themselves. To this end, she always saw the best in everyone and remarked kindly upon it" (156). Because Melanie marries Ashley, Scarlett sees her as a rival—even an enemy. But Melanie consistently shows love to Scarlett, defending her character even when everyone else turns against her. At the end, when Melanie is dying, Scarlett finally sees Melanie as a redeemer: "Never before had it occurred to her that she needed Melanie. But now, the truth surged in, down to the deepest recesses of her soul. She had relied on Melanie, even as she had relied upon herself, and she had never known it. Now, Melanie was dying and Scarlett knew she could not get along without her. Now, as she tiptoed across the room toward the quiet figure, panic clutching at her heart, she knew that Melanie had been her sword and her shield, her comfort and her strength" (1008–09). In a novel mostly devoid of Christian or biblical references, the biblical allusions at the end of this passage clearly put Melanie in the role of a savior. More biblical allusions appear shortly afterward: "Rhett's words came back to her again, 'She loves you. Let that be your cross.' Well, the cross was heavier now. It was bad enough that she had tried by every art to take Ashley from her. But now it was worse that Melanie, who had trusted her blindly through life, was laying the same love and trust on her in death" (1011). Melanie gives sacrificial love, even as she is dying. And her death finally gives Scarlett self-knowledge to understand that her supposed love for Ashley was a sham and that her real love is for Rhett: "She had thought, half an hour ago, that she had lost everything in the world, except money, everything that made life desirable, Ellen, Gerald, Bonnie, Mammy, Melanie and Ashley. She had to lose them all to realize that she loved Rhett" (1022). This passage echoes Jesus's claim that "whoever desires to save his life will lose it, but whoever loses his life for My sake will find it" (Matt 16:25). The sacrificial death of the redeemer Melanie allows Scarlett to die to herself so that she can receive new life.

However, in the final chapter, Mitchell rejects this Christian story of redemption for an ironic story of failed redemption. Although the Bible asserts that "love never fails" (1 Cor 13:8), Rhett tells her that "even the most deathless love could wear out" (1029). Instead of redeeming love, Scarlett is left with one of the most famous rejections in literature: "My dear, I don't give a damn" (1035). And instead of a reborn and redeemed Scarlett, the novel ends with only a vague hope: "I'll think of it all tomorrow, at Tara. I can stand it then. Tomorrow, I'll think of some way to get him back. After all, tomorrow is another day" (1037). "Tomorrow," of course, opens another possibility for redemption (not to mention a sequel), but it is an unfulfilled potential in the novel.

This conclusion annuls Melanie's redemptive death. Perhaps Mitchell used this ending to open up the possibility of a sequel, but within the structure of the novel as it stands, readers are left with a failure of redemption, a tragic loss of almost everything and everyone close to Scarlett, with only a hope that the protagonist has at last achieved some self-knowledge and may yet receive redemption (Rhett's love) and the happiness that she could not obtain through money or manipulation. This ending suggests that literature may be structured upon not only a pattern of redemption but also upon an antithetical pattern of "antiredemption." As I have already shown, this was a significant element in the structure of *Uncle Tom's Cabin*. In *Gone with the Wind*, it seems to be a controlling pattern. In the next chapter, I will argue that is the pattern for a distinct genre and literary experience of its own.

## *VALLEY OF THE DOLLS*

The same kind of structure—repeatedly offering potential redeemers only to have each one fail—characterizes Jacqueline Susann's *Valley of the Dolls*. The novel follows three young, beautiful women—Jennifer, Neely, and Anne—as they search for redeemer husbands. Jennifer's mother, desperate for money, had sent her to school in Europe and pushed her to marry a rich husband. After a lesbian relationship and an annulled marriage to an Italian prince who turned out to be broke, Jennifer marries a rich singer named Tony Polar. She believes that now her life can be secure and happy: "It wasn't just his money and security she wanted. She also wanted to be a good wife. She wanted a child."[49] She soon learns that he is frequently unfaithful to her and that he has a congenital, progressive mental disability. She aborts a pregnancy and divorces him. Years later, she says to Anne, "I'd give my life for someone who would just love me" (288). Finally, she believes that she has found real love with Senator Winston Adams. But before they can marry, she learns that she has breast cancer and needs a mastectomy. Fearing that Adams will not love her without her beauty intact, she commits suicide, leaving a note to him saying, "Thanks for making it almost come true" (307). Every potential redeemer had failed her.

Neely was orphaned when young and had grown up with a struggling Vaudeville act. When she suddenly achieves stardom on Broadway and in the movies, she marries then quickly divorces a public relations agent named Mel and a famous designer named Ted. After a failed suicide and years of self-destructive behavior, she believes that the right man can save her: "I want a guy. And I'm gonna be choosy from now on. . . . I want someone who cares about me, someone I can respect . . . someone to Love" (373). Like Jennifer, she seems to believe that security and happiness will come from a husband. But in the end, after an affair with the husband of her friend Anne, she relapses into her self-destructive use of drugs and alcohol and intolerable self-centeredness.

Anne seems to come the closest to finding her husband-redeemer. Leaving behind a stifling small-town culture, she comes to New York City and immediately finds a good job and a wealthy man who wants to marry her. However, she realizes that money

49. Susann, *Valley of the Dolls*, 182.

alone cannot save her. She tells her suitor, "I don't want to get married—until I fall in love. And I *do* want to fall in love . . . , I want that desperately. And I want children. I want a daughter. I want to love her . . . be close to her" (97–98). Soon she meets and falls in love with a man named Lyon Burke: "The most important thing in the world had happened. She knew the feeling of love—and she knew it was the whole reason for living" (116). But Lyon leaves her, and she has a long affair with an older man. Just as they are about to marry, Lyon returns, and she drops her wedding plans. With Lyon, she believes, "This was complete fulfillment. When she held him in her arms she suddenly knew it was important to love—more important than *being* loved" (348). Lyon marries Anne, but in the end, after Lyon has affairs with her friend Neely and with another actress, Anne realizes that "she would love Lyon less, until one day there would be nothing left—no hurt, and no love" (407). She has "everything she had ever wanted" (407), but her life remains unfulfilled, and she turns to drugs for comfort.

Both *Gone with the Wind* and *Valley of the Dolls* play with the readers' expectations, built over at least two hundred years of romance novels, that these women will find happiness and fulfillment once they find the right man. In the postromantic twentieth century, both novels pointedly debunk those expectations. But both novels would be impossible without these expectations of redemption. Although these two best sellers do not simply fulfill readers' expectations of redemption, they illustrate how important the pattern of redemption can be even when it is not fulfilled. The following chapters will show how entire genres of literature come from the particular ways that stories manipulate this pattern.

# 4

## Antiredemption

### "THE CASK OF AMONTILLADO"

READERS LOOKING for this pattern of divine redemption in literature may be affected as much by its absence as by its presence, especially when there is a deliberate antiredemptive construction. For example, few would claim that Poe's "The Cask of Amontillado" is a Christian story or even that it is built around a redeemer. Although Poe comes from a Christian culture and sets his story in a Christian culture, he does not seem to portray Christian themes or values. Love, forgiveness, and redemption are not apparent in the story. However, it is this very absence of redemption that gives the story its horrific power.

The opening sentence reveals man's lost condition at its worst: "The thousand injuries of Fortunato I had borne as best I could, but when he ventured upon insult I vowed revenge."[1] Fortunato has done wrong, and Montresor will wrong him in return. Montresor not only refuses to suffer for the good of Fortunato—he will not even suffer for harming him: "A wrong is unredressed when retribution overtakes its redresser" (70). In the end, Fortunato has died for his "sin," and Montresor glories in his vengeance. This story seems to follow a pattern that is the very opposite of redemption.

---

1. Poe, *The Collected Tales and Poems*, 70.

Poe provides clues that this "antiredemption" is deliberate. His characters' names, for instance, suggest chance—Fortunato ("fortunate")—and selfishness—Montresor ("my treasure"): clearly not redemptive values. Montresor's coat of arms makes the point even more forcefully. It is "A huge human foot . . . ; the foot crushes a serpent rampant whose fangs are embedded in the heel," with the motto, "Nemo me impune lacessit" (72). The fact that the serpent—an obvious allusion to Satan—is "rampant" suggests that it may be the serpent saying, "No one provokes me with impunity" as it buries its fangs in the provoking heel. Here we see the antithesis of the "proto-evangel" of Genesis 3:15, where God tells the serpent, "I will put enmity between you and the woman, and between your seed and her Seed; he shall bruise your head, and you shall bruise His heel." Traditional Christian interpretation has seen this as a prophecy that Jesus, the seed of the woman, would defeat Satan, the serpent, when Satan caused Jesus's death. But Poe seems to present Montresor as the victorious serpent.

This inversion of the gospel reaches a climax at the tomb. In the Gospels, Jesus the innocent Redeemer dies to pay for sin, is placed dead in the tomb, and leaves the empty tomb alive as a sign of his ultimate victory over sin and death. In contrast, in "The Cask of Amontillado," Fortunato the sinner is placed alive in the tomb, dies there, and remains in the tomb as a sign of Montresor the serpent's ultimate victory. Fortunato's last words are, "*For the love of God, Montresor!*" (74). Montresor's sarcastic repetition—"Yes, . . . for the love of God" (just before sealing the tomb)— ironically negates the love of God and annihilates any hope of redemption.

The horror of Poe's story resonates with audiences because he presents the opposite of the human desire for redemption. Although most readers are probably not consciously aware of this pattern of antiredemption, they feel its force. Few would call "The Cask of Amontillado" a great work of literature in the way that *Hamlet* is a great work, but it is memorable in much the same way that villains like Iago in *Othello* and Richard III are memorable:

because they so thoroughly negate the redemption that people need and desire.

## FRANKENSTEIN

A similar analysis explains the success of the best-known horror story in the English language: Mary Shelley's *Frankenstein*. Victor Frankenstein takes upon himself the role of God when he creates a human life. That life, like all postlapsarian human life, is flawed— monstrous—and in need of redemption. If the story were a comedy, Victor would overcome difficulties and find a way to make the creature good. (See Mel Brooks's film *Young Frankenstein*.) If it were a tragedy, he would give his own life to make the monster good or at least to bring goodness to the world by destroying the monster. But the horror of the story is that there is no redemption. Victor's friends and family try to redeem him with their love for him, but the monster kills them. After his loved ones are dead, Victor dies in a vain attempt to kill the monster. Victor is lost; the monster is lost; and the very world may finally be saved from the rampages of the monster only by the monster's claim that he will take his own life: the only twisted sort of redemption offered by the novel. Such a failure of redemption is the essence of horror.

The fallen nature of this novel's world is made clear in one of Victor Frankenstein's first statements when he tells the narrator Walton, "You have hope and the world before you, and have no cause for despair. But I—I have lost everything, and cannot begin life anew."[2] Like Poe, Shelley uses a biblical, Genesis 3 allusion to reinforce this state of loss when Frankenstein then tells Walton, "I ardently hope that the gratification of your wishes may not be a serpent to sting you, as mine has been to me" (14). Frankenstein's youth had been idyllic, almost Edenic. He says, "No youth could have passed more happily than mine" (21), and he describes his family as "our domestic circle, from which care and pain seemed

2. Shelley, *Frankenstein*, 13.

forever banished" (25). To preserve this unfallen state, he attempts to take on qualities of deity and to be a creator of life: "What glory would attend the discovery, if I could banish disease from the human frame, and render man invulnerable to any but violent death! . . . A new species would bless me as its creator and source; many happy and excellent natures would owe their being to me" (23, 37). Naturally, such hubris is doomed. Immediately upon the creation of his "new species," he recognizes his failure: "How can I describe my emotions at this catastrophe, or how delineate the wretch whom, with such infinite pains and care, I had endeavored to form?" (40). Shelley again uses an allusion to reinforce the fallenness of this creation: "it became a thing such as even Dante could not have conceived" (41). After the monster murders Victor's little brother William, Victor foresees his doom: "I foresaw obscurely that I was destined to become the most wretched of human beings. Alas! I prophesied truly, and failed only in one single circumstance,—that, in all the misery I imagined and dreaded, I did not conceive the hundredth part of the anguish that I was destined to endure" (58–59).

From this point on, there are multiple failures of redemption in the novel. For example, the servant girl Justine is executed for William's murder. Victor, who knows that she is innocent, cannot produce evidence to redeem her, and because she is framed by the monster, who had himself committed the murder, her innocent sacrifice is not redemptive but bitterly ironic. Next, when Victor's eventual fiancée Elizabeth sees his despairing reaction to the execution of Justine, she offers herself: "Be calm my dear Victor: I would sacrifice my life to your peace" (77). This offer, too, leads to bitter irony when Victor expects to be killed by the monster on his wedding night, and the monster instead strangles Elizabeth. Her death in his place thus leads not to his peace but to overwhelming grief and despair.

Perhaps the ultimate failed redemption in the story is not that of Victor or of his friends and family but that of the monster, who clearly recognizes his own fallen state. Based on his reading of *Paradise Lost*, he tells Victor, "Remember, that I am thy creature: I ought to be thy Adam; but I am rather the fallen angel, whom thou drivest from joy for no misdeed" (84). Childlike and innocent but deformed and ugly, the monster tries to be good and to find companionship, but he is thwarted at every turn. After observing and secretly helping the De Lacey family for months, he attempts to befriend them but is violently driven off as soon as they see him. Later, he saves a young girl from drowning but is shot as a result. He says, "This was, then, the reward of my benevolence! I had saved a human being from destruction, and, as a recompense, I now writhed under the pain of a wound, which shattered the flesh and bone" (128). He tries to be a redeemer, but such repeated rejections transform him into an antiredeemer, filled with "hellish rage and gnashing of teeth." He vows "eternal hatred and vengeance to all mankind" (128). Focusing his vengeance particularly on Victor, he tells him, "I will work at your destruction, nor finish until I desolate your heart, so that you curse the hour of your birth" (133).

The balance of the novel, then, is the mortal struggle between Victor and his monster. The monster demands the creation of a spouse as the price of peace, but Victor eventually refuses. On a theoretical level, perhaps the novel thus shows that redemption cannot be purchased by creation: only innocent suffering can bring true redemption. After Victor aborts the creation of the monster's spouse, the monster kills Clerval, Victor's closest friend, and Elizabeth, his bride. He then leads Victor for months in a vain chase, taunting him and luring him finally to the frozen Arctic Ocean. There the explorer/narrator Walton finds Victor and learns his story. While dying, Victor explains to Walton that both he and the monster are lost: "Miserable himself, that he may render no other wretched he ought to die. The task of his destruction was mine, but I have failed" (210). Not only does Victor fail as a redeemer, he cannot even fulfill the kind of cleansing vengeance achieved by Hamlet or Oedipus.

At the conclusion, the monster likewise summarizes the devastation of his own life to Walton: "The fallen angel becomes a malignant devil. Yet even that enemy of God and man had friends and associates in his desolation: I am quite alone" (214). He tells Walton that he will go to "the most northern extremity of the globe" and incinerate himself (215). In the last line of the novel, he is "lost in darkness and distance" (216). Thus, *Frankenstein* presents a world of struggle, suffering, evil, and emptiness, devoid of any redemption. The essence of horror is the absence of redemption.

## L'ÉTRANGER

In the twentieth century, such antiredemption has become even more prevalent—even dominating certain types of literature. The French existentialists, such as Sartre and Camus, seem to have delighted in thumbing their figurative noses at Christian hopes for redemption. Sartre's famous play *Huis Clos* (English title, *No Exit*) portrays a naturalistic hell in which people endlessly torment one another.

Camus's *L'étranger* (*The Outsider*) even more deliberately renounces redemption. The story begins with death: "Today, Mama died. Or maybe yesterday: I don't know."[3] The protagonist, Meursault moves through a hedonistic world of sensations, eventually killing a man "because of the sun" (147). He grudgingly half admits the (Christian) position that his very nature is sinful: "I did not very well understand how the qualities of an ordinary man could become the overwhelming charges against a culprit" (142). And eventually he is condemned to death not so much for murder as for his failure to cry at his mother's funeral: "What does it matter if, being accused of murder, he was executed for not having cried at his mother's burial?" (170).

Yet Mersault is offered redemptive possibilities at several points in the novel. Before he commits the murder, his mistress,

---

3. Camus, *L'étranger*, 9; my translation throughout.

Marie, offers him human love, but he rejects it: "She asked me if I loved her. I answered her that it didn't mean anything but that it seemed to me that I didn't" (54). Similarly, his boss offers him a new job far away in Paris, but he is not interested: "He asked me then if I wasn't interested in a change of life. I answered that one never changes one's life" (62). After the murder, the redemptive offers become overtly Christian. In a pretrial interrogation, a judge places a silver crucifix in front of Meursault:

> "Do you recognize this?"
>
> I said, "Yes, naturally."
>
> Then he said to me very fast and in an impassioned way that he believed in God, that his conviction was that no man was so guilty that God would not pardon him, but that this required that a man by his repentance become like a child, of whom the soul is empty and ready to welcome everything. . . . He exhorted me one last time . . . asking me if I believed in God. I said I didn't. . . . But across the table, he was already pushing forward the Christ under my eyes and crying in an unreasonable way, "Me, I am a Christian. I ask this One to pardon your faults. How can you not believe that he suffered for you?"
>
> I noticed that he was addressing me informally, but . . . also, I had enough of it. . . .
>
> To my surprise, he cried triumphantly: "You see, you see," he was saying. "Do you believe, and will you trust in Him?"
>
> Evidently, I said no one more time. He fell back onto his armchair. (98–100)

Finally, after Meursault refuses several times to see the prison chaplain, the chaplain comes to him anyway. In a long passage that all but ends the novel, he tries to persuade Meursault to believe in God. Meursault finally drives him off with a harangue asserting that he has lived his life and that nothing matters to him. He concludes with the wish that there might be many spectators at his execution "and that they might welcome me with cries of hate" (172).

Camus has thus deliberately rejected—even poked fun at—the idea that redemption is possible. His protagonist claims, "I was guilty, I was paying, one could ask no more of me" (165). Most readers find this unsatisfying, even disturbing. Whether Camus's position is existentialist, nihilistic, or merely realistic, its literary value comes primarily from its power to shock. Readers remember it because it disrupts their expectations or because the language and the protagonist are so well created. But few readers would say that they "enjoy" the story of *L'étranger*. As with Poe's "Cask of Amontillado" and Shelley's *Frankenstein*, readers find that the absence or rejection of redemption gives the story a kind of power, but it is a fearful power.

## AND THEN THERE WERE NONE

A best-selling story by Agatha Christie provides a fascinating opportunity to compare the effects of redemptive and antiredemptive plot structures. Christie's *And Then There Were None* claims as many as 100 million in sales. (The novel was first published in 1939 as *Ten Little Niggers*, then in America as *Ten Little Indians*, then as *And Then There Were None*, and finally as *The Nursery Rhyme Murders*.) There are a stage version written by Christie and at least two movie versions.[4] In many ways, this is a story of vengeance more than of redemption. In fact, the original novel is a tale of antiredemption. All ten major characters except one, Judge Wargrave, are guilty of some form of murder, and in the end, after all the guilty characters have been killed, Judge Wargrave takes his own life. No one is saved; no one dies for anyone else. The antiredemptive story is bleak and horrifying.

However, the stage version is very different. All ten characters are again accused of murder, but this time only eight of them are ultimately killed, once again as judgment for their crimes. However, in the end, two characters survive, both of whom are portrayed as innocent. As in the novel, Vera Claythorne is accused of allowing a young boy to drown so that her lover could receive

---

4. Robyns, *The Mystery of Agatha Christie*, 170–71.

his inheritance, and Philip Lombard is accused of leaving the African soldiers under his command to die in the bush.[5] But this time, in the final scene, Vera reveals that it was her lover who had caused the boy's death while she had done all she could to try to save him. And Lombard, who had publicly admitted to his crime earlier, reveals privately that he had actually done all he could to try to save his soldiers.[6]

What brings this version of the story quite close to the pattern of Christian redemption is that Lombard "dies" and then saves Vera. When only these two characters remain, each believes, by process of elimination, that the other must have killed the other eight characters. Vera grabs Lombard's pistol and shoots him in self-defense. After his apparent death, Judge Wargrave, who had staged his own fake death, reappears, reveals that he has killed the other seven, and prepares to kill Vera. At the last moment, Lombard revives, grabs his pistol, and shoots Wargrave. An innocent victim dies, returns to life, and saves another character from death. Although this equals neither the substitutionary death of Sydney Carton for the Darnays in *A Tale of Two Cities* nor Frodo's self-sacrificing struggle to save Middle Earth from the Dark Lord Sauron, it does employ most of the pattern of the sacrificial, redemptive savior.[7]

## BELOVED

Another pair of texts that can illustrate the differing effects of redemptive and antiredemptive structures is Harriet Beecher Stowe's *Uncle Tom's Cabin* and Toni Morrison's *Beloved*. On the surface, these two novels reveal obvious points of comparison and

5. Christie, *The Mousetrap and Other Plays*, 18.

6. Ibid., 69–70.

7. Because this story has both redemptive and antiredemptive versions, it would be very helpful if the sales of and audience reactions to the different versions could be traced. While other antiredemptive stories have had some popularity as horror stories, I hypothesize that the redemptive version of this story has augmented its popularity.

contrast. In comparison, both attack slavery and deal with racial issues. Both use a setting focused on, though ranging away from, the Kentucky-Ohio border region. Both include a key scene of a young slave woman escaping across the Ohio River with a child. Both include strong spiritual elements. Both are by women. In contrast, one is written and set before the end of slavery while the other is written more than a century later and focuses primarily on the aftermath of slavery. One emphasizes the experience of a man (Uncle Tom); the other, a woman (Sethe). One author is white; the other is black. But the essential difference in the two stories lies in their uses of redemption.

*Uncle Tom's Cabin* was discussed in detail in the previous chapter, but, in review, its structure is thoroughly redemptive. Innocent characters risk or give their lives to save others, and the deaths of little Eva St. Clare and of Uncle Tom not only rescue others but bring them outright to salvation in the Christian sense. *Uncle Tom's Cabin* is simply, even blatantly, *about* redemption. This simplicity makes the novel easy to understand and seems to have contributed to its immense popularity. Even today, after more than one hundred and thirty years, although few people read it, it remains a cultural icon, recognizable to most Americans. However, it is not today widely considered to be "great literature," perhaps largely because of its lack of subtlety and complexity.

*Beloved*, on the other hand, is a far more complex work, and much of its structural complexity comes from its convoluted employment of redemption. It reveals fallenness that needs redemption on multiple levels. First, the slaveholding/racist white American culture is evil and must be redeemed: Sethe's mother-in-law, Baby Suggs, dies saying, "There is no bad luck in the world but whitefolks."[8] Second, Baby Suggs, Paul D, Sethe, and all the other slaves need to be literally and emotionally redeemed from slavery. Third, Beloved was killed by her mother as an infant and needs redemption from death. Above all, Sethe must be redeemed from

8. Morrison, *Beloved*, 89.

her past in slavery and her murder of her own infant, Beloved. The novel deals with all of these using a mixture of redemptions and antiredemptions.

White culture, for instance, remains mostly evil and un-redeemed, but at the very end Mr. Bodwin, the white man who owns the house where Sethe lives, does not press charges against Sethe for trying to kill him with an ice pick. One of the blacks responds, "That be just like him, too. He's somebody never turned us down. Steady as a rock" (265). Thus, there is at least one white who faces death and shows forgiveness and goodness. Likewise, Amy Denver, a poor white girl, rescues Sethe as she is escaping from slavery and going into labor. So there is a very limited re-demption for white culture.

All of the slaves in the novel are freed from slavery, but they are freed in diverse ways. Baby Suggs's son Halle purchases her freedom by working beyond his own slavery, on Sundays and holi-days, providing a literal and sacrificial redemption. The result of her redemption is her joyful preaching as "Baby Suggs, holy" (87–89), and she proclaims to the blacks who come to her clearing "that the only grace they could have was the grace they could imagine" (88). Later, however, the coming of the whites to her home to reclaim Sethe and her children into slavery and Sethe's murder of her child to avoid slavery destroy Baby Suggs's "grace": "Her faith, her love, her imagination and her great big old heart began to collapse" (89). Although she had been redeemed from slavery to the whites, she realizes that "those white things have taken all I had or dreamed" (89), and so her redemption is undone, and she dies. Similar failed redemptions destroy Baby Suggs's son Halle, who tries to escape slavery but goes mad after helplessly watching his master's sons sexually abuse his wife Sethe, and fellow slave Sixo, who is burned and shot to death for trying to escape. Even those who escape, such as Paul D and Sethe's children Howard, Buglar, and Denver, end up drifting aimlessly or otherwise isolated and lost. Their past and the evil white culture around them entrap them.

Ultimately, however, the story is about Sethe and her daughter Beloved, and their relationship displays the complexity of the possibilities of redemption. After Sethe's three children escape, she tries to flee as well, although she is pregnant. She suffers and nearly dies, but with the help of a white girl and a free black man, she gives birth to Denver and escapes to rejoin her children at Baby Suggs's home in Ohio. When her owner tracks her down and invades Baby's home to capture Sethe and her children, Sethe tries to kill all four children rather than let them be taken back into slavery. She succeeds only in killing her unnamed toddler daughter, later named Beloved. This desperate act convinces her owner that she is insane and worthless as a slave, so he abandons his claim to her and her children. Thus, the sacrifice of the innocent victim Beloved redeems Sethe and her other children from slavery. However, Beloved was not a willing victim, so the redemption was not a true redemption. (Sethe says, "I took one journey and I paid for the ticket, but . . . it cost too much!" [15].) Because Sethe's act ruins the trust of her other children, Howard and Buglar leave home, and Denver becomes isolated and, for a time, deaf and dumb. Beloved becomes a ghost haunting the house where Sethe, Denver, and Baby Suggs live, and the house becomes a place of isolation and sterility where there are "no visitors of any sort and certainly no friends" (12).

When Paul D arrives at the house after eighteen years, he comes as a possible redeemer. His own escape from slavery involved years of terrible suffering, and the narrator says, "he had become the kind of man who could walk into a house and make the women cry. Because with him, in his presence, they could. There was something blessed in his manner" (17). As soon as he begins to build a relationship with Sethe, the ghost of Beloved reacts by shaking the entire house, but Paul D violently exorcises it. Then, when his presence seems to be bringing healing to Sethe and Denver, Beloved appears as an eighteen-year-old girl.

Beloved is therefore an innocent victim who died to bring redemption and returned to life in bodily form. But her sacrifice was not voluntary, and she comes not giving life but taking love and life from those who benefited from her death. Paul D suffered to try to achieve his own redemption and comes offering love. But he has not received true redemption from his own past of shame and suffering, and he comes unable to give his own, still-lost self to save Sethe. Sethe had paid "too much" for her own redemption, but she had given Beloved's life, not her own. Ironically, she now needs to be redeemed from her act of redemption. Like Paul D, she has not received true redemption from her past of shame and suffering and cannot give her lost life to save others. A hopeless situation is established that appears resolvable only through tragic loss (a character dying for his or her own partial redemption) or horror (failed redemption). In particular, if Beloved could succeed in taking or taking over Sethe's life, the novel would be a true horror story with Beloved the antiredeemer destroying the others. As Sethe's daughter Denver realizes, "Sethe was trying to make up for the handsaw [used to kill Beloved]; Beloved was making her pay for it" (251).

Instead, Morrison creates a redemptive community. It is the entire black community that has suffered innocently in America and so can redeem Paul D, Sethe, and perhaps even Beloved. First, a minor character with a literally redemptive name—Stamp Paid—finds Paul D, who has abandoned Sethe and her home, driven away by Beloved. Paul D is living, appropriately, at the Church of the Holy Redeemer (218). There, Paul D is able to deal with "the loss of a red, red heart" (235) and return to Sethe. Next, Denver, the one character who does not carry the burden and shame of a past in slavery (she was born as Sethe was escaping), reaches out to the community for help: "She would have to leave behind the yard; step off the edge of the world, . . . and go ask somebody for help" (243). Her quest for help brings the community of black women together: "Maybe they were sorry for her. Or for Sethe. Maybe they were sorry for the years of their own disdain. Maybe they were simply nice people who could hold meanness toward each other for just so long and when trouble rode bareback among them, quickly, easily they did what they could to trip him up" (249). Denver's self-sacrificial act brings together thirty women who come to save Sethe. They "could not countenance the possibility of sin moving on in the house, unleashed and sassy" (256). As they arrive at Sethe's home, they begin to pray. The sound of their prayers and incantations "broke over Sethe and she trembled like the baptized in its wash" (261). Finally, Mr. Bodwin (the good white man: "Steady as a rock" [265]) appears among the women, and Sethe, mistaking him for the white master who came to capture her and her children eighteen years earlier, rushes at him to kill him. This is the action she should have taken eighteen years earlier to sacrifice herself for her children. Now, however, with slavery gone and Mr. Bodwin innocent, her mistaken act could only create a final failed redemption. But Denver and the women stop her. Beloved, now separated from Sethe and exorcised by the women, finally is destroyed: "Disappeared, some say, exploded right before their eyes" (263).

It is, therefore, the black community that has suffered, forgiven, and brought redemption: "Some brought what they could and what they believed would work. Stuffed in apron pockets, strung around their necks, lying in the space between their breasts. Others brought Christian faith—as shield and sword. Most brought a little of both" (257). Even so, Sethe is freed but not filled with new life. Because she has now lost Beloved—her "best thing" (272)—she is unredeemed and remains in the bed where Baby Suggs had given up on life and died. But Paul D comes, having experienced "the miracle" (269) and brings with him "the blessedness, that has made him the kind of man who can walk in a house and make the women cry" (272). He gives her back the life she had lost: "You your best thing, Seethe. You are" (273). Sethe is redeemed. In the end then, the past is paid for, and new life is given. Paul D tells Sethe, "me and you, we got more yesterday than anybody. We need some kind of tomorrow" (273). Although this is not a novel like *Uncle Tom's Cabin* about simple and obvious redemption, it ultimately brings the reader though layers of cultural and individual antiredemption to what is essentially a comic ending.

⌒

Identifying the multiple kinds and acts of redemption in a story reveals how that story achieves its complex effects on readers. Although the most popular novels seem to be those that follow a straightforward pattern of redemption, powerful literary effects can be achieved—as in works like *Frankenstein*, *L'étranger*, and *Beloved*—by negating that pattern in various ways. Such variations have become the norm in most postmodern and postcolonial novels, as I will show in the next chapter.

# 5

## Postcolonial Literature

U P TO this point, most of the literature covered in this study has been ancient or Western. Such literature may carry a hidden cultural bias toward redemptive themes. In particular, Western literature from Augustine through the nineteenth century was often dominated by a Christian worldview and often openly proclaimed Christian doctrine. In America especially, well into the nineteenth century the best-selling books were frequently Christian books: from *Pilgrim's Progress* and *The Day of Doom* to *Uncle Tom's Cabin* and *Ben-Hur*. However, by the middle of the twentieth century, Christian books were largely relegated to a marginal status, published and sold by Christians for Christians, while the mainstream of literature largely ignored or mocked Christianity. Therefore, to explore whether the pattern of redemption is really essential to all literature, it should be useful to examine literature from non-Christian and post-Christian cultures.

Postcolonial and postmodern works of literature often deliberately reject and even mock expectations of redemption. Typically they present a world in which "things fall apart," without any climactic act of redemption. Yet such works often seem to raise the possibility of redemption quite deliberately, as if to emphasize what's missing. Such works as Gabriel García Márquez's *One Hundred Years of Solitude*, Salman Rushdie's *Midnight's Children*,

Chinua Achebe's *Things Fall Apart*, and Khaled Hosseini's *The Kite Runner* all follow this pattern.

## ONE HUNDRED YEARS OF SOLITUDE

For example, García Márquez's *One Hundred Years of Solitude*, as a seminal work of magical realism, helped to establish some of the key themes and techniques of postmodernism: absurdism, unstable notions of character and plot, and deconstruction of its own premises. Throughout the text, it continually sets up but then disappoints expectations of redemption. The opening statement, for example, indicates a possible redeemer: "Many years later, as he faced the firing squad, Colonel Aureliano Buendía was to remember that distant afternoon when his father took him to discover ice."[1] Readers therefore expect this central character to die for something, redeeming a friend or a cause. This feeling is reinforced as the firing squad is mentioned repeatedly (55, 88, 96, 103, 114), and finally he does face the firing squad as a leader of the Liberal revolutionary forces. But his brother José Arcadio threatens the firing squad, and they spare Colonel Aureliano Buendía, changing sides and following him as he assumes command of the revolution (141). Eventually the revolution becomes meaningless, as he recognizes "that all we're fighting for is power" (182).

By the end of his life, he seems to be beyond redemption: "Then he made one last effort to search in his heart for the place where his affection had rotted away and he could not find it" (188). He attempts suicide by shooting himself through the chest but cannot die (193). Near the end of his life, his own mother, Ursula, "reached the conclusion that the son for whom she would have given her life was simply a man incapable of love" (267). When finally death comes, there is no redemption: "Then he went to the chestnut tree, thinking about the circus, and while he urinated he tried to keep on thinking about the circus, but he could no longer

1. García Márquez, *One Hundred Years of Solitude*, 1.

find the memory. He pulled his head in between his shoulders like a baby chick and remained motionless with his forehead against the trunk of the chestnut tree (287). He dies a meaningless death in his old age.

Other potential redeemers likewise come to meaningless ends. Ursula, the matriarch of the Buendía family, tries to save her family. As mentioned above, "she would have given her life" for her son Aureliano (267), and she repeatedly tries to save her family, but she comes to wonder "if that madhouse which had cost her so many headaches . . . was destined to become a trash heap of perdition" (269). She goes on to wonder "if it was not preferable to lie down once and for all in her grave and let them throw the earth over her, and she asked God, without fear, if he really believed that people were made of iron in order to bear so many troubles and mortifications" (270). When she does die, there is a deliberate hint of redemption in her parallel with Jesus Christ: "They found her dead on the morning of Good Friday" (369). But the only thing that follows her death is a plague in which "the birds in their confusion were running into walls like clay pigeons and breaking through screens to die in the bedrooms" (369). There is no redemption here.

Like Ursula, the seventeen sons of Colonel Aureliano Buendía have a parallel with Christ: stigmata in the shape of crosses indelibly marked on their foreheads at an Ash Wednesday service. When the colonel sees an innocent child and grandfather decapitated by a policeman, he reaches "the limits of atonement" and calls upon these sons to right the wrong: " 'One of these days,' he shouted, 'I'm going to arm my boys so we can get rid of these shitty gringos!'" (257). However, instead of bringing salvation, the seventeen are "hunted down like rabbits" (257). There is no redemption here.

Another member of the Buendía family, Remedios the Beauty, shows innocence and supernatural beauty and is said to be "not a creature of this world" (213). However, rather than being a redeemer, she "possessed the powers of death" (253), causing men around her to die in despair. She ultimately ascends, much like Jesus, into the air (while folding Brabant sheets in the garden, 254–55). Yet she comes to a meaningless end: "lost forever . . . in the upper atmosphere where not even the highest-flying birds of memory could reach her" (255). One of her nephews, the fourth Buendía to be named José Arcadio, is supposed to be destined to become Pope, but he returns from his training in Rome as a wastrel and ends up drowned in a pool of champagne by four children whom he had corrupted. There is no redemption here.

In the final two chapters, it seems as if the Buendía family and the world of Macondo might be redeemed by the love of the last two Buendías, Amaranta Ursula and the twentieth by the name of Aureliano. Amaranta Ursula "returned with the first angels of December" (405) and brought new life to the house. Her husband leaves her, and she and Aureliano fall in love: "both of them remained floating in an empty universe where the only everyday and eternal reality was love" (437). They believe in the power of their love to redeem them even from death: "They learned that dominant obsessions can prevail against death and they were happy again with the certainty that they would go on loving each other in their shape as apparitions long after other species of future animals would steal from the insects the paradise of misery that the insects were finally stealing from man" (442). When they have a child, Amaranta Ursula believes that he is "predisposed to begin the race again from the beginning and cleanse it of its pernicious vices and solitary calling, for he was the only one in a century who had been engendered with love" (442). But he is born of incest with a foretold curse—the tail of a pig. Amaranta Ursula bleeds to death, and the infant is devoured by ants. Aureliano ends in a solipsistic vision: "For it was foreseen that the city of mirrors (or mirages) would be wiped out by the wind and exiled from the memory of men at the precise moment when Aureliano Babilonia would finish deciphering the parchments, and that everything written on them was unrepeatable since time immemorial and forever more, because races condemned to one hundred years of solitude did not have a second opportunity on earth" (448).

Though filled with a host of potential redeemers, the novel ends in meaningless absurdity. In this postmodern world, there is "no second opportunity on earth," and redemption is an empty and impossible illusion.

## MIDNIGHT'S CHILDREN

Salman Rushdie's *Midnight's Children* likewise presents multiple possibilities for redemption, none of which is ultimately fulfilled. The most obvious of the potential redeemers is the narrator himself, Saleem Sinai. A holy man appears just before Saleem's birth and says, "I have come to await the coming of the One. The Mubarak—He who is Blessed."[2] Saleem also recounts that, even as a baby, "I was already beginning to take my place at the center of the universe; and by the time I had finished, I would give meaning to it all" (143–44). As he grows, he tries to hold to this hope, but by age nine, he begins to doubt his redemptive ability: "I became afraid that everyone was wrong—that my much-trumpeted existence might turn out to be utterly useless, void, and without the shred of a purpose" (173). Saleem's doubts are later reinforced by his alter ego Shiva (who had been switched with Saleem at birth): "For what reason you're rich and I'm poor? Where's the reason in starving, man? God knows how many millions of damn fools living in this country, man, and you think there's a purpose! Man, I'll tell you—you got to get what you can, do what you can with it, and then you got to die" (252). Saleem the narrator repeatedly tries to save his homeland, India, and give meaning to India's history, and repeatedly he comes up against random events and meaningless violence and death.

From a narrative perspective, Saleem's redemptive failures may be a result of his passivity. He asserts, "I've been the sort of person

2. Rushdie, *Midnight's Children*, 126.

*to whom things have been done*; but Saleem Sinai, perennial victim, persists in seeing himself as protagonist" (273). If the very notion of plot—resolution of a problem—implies a redemptive pattern, such passivity may be antithetical to redemption. Where there is no willed action, there are only random events. Although my proposed paradigm of redemption centers on an innocent victim who willingly suffers to save others, if that suffering is purely passive, then the victim is a mere scapegoat. The perfect redeemer actively offers himself or herself as a sacrifice.[3] Postmodern and postcolonial literature frequently foregrounds the social forces that constrain the individual. Therefore, the ultimate goal of such literature may be to highlight the forces that work to thwart the redeemer.

Saleem Sinai sees these forces and hopes to overcome them through his Midnight's Children Conference (MCC): a telepathic congregation of all the children born in India at the hour of Indian independence. When he sees this Conference breaking down, he cries out, "Brothers, sisters! . . . Do not let this happen! Do not permit the endless duality of masses-and-classes, capital-and-labor, them-and-us to come between us! We . . . must be a third principle, we must be the force which drives between the horns of the dilemma; for only by being other, by being new, can we fulfill the promise of our birth!" (292). Saleem hopes "to save the country" (444) through the supernatural powers of the 581 children of the MCC, but instead his alter ego Shiva leads the dissolution of the Conference and ultimately tracks them all down so that "The Widow" (representing Indira Ghandi when she seized Emergency powers in India) can kill or castrate them.

In the end, Saleem persists in hoping that he can redeem his own (and India's) story from absurdity: "The art is to change the flavor in degree, but not in kind: and above all . . . to give it shape and form—that is to say, meaning. (I have mentioned my fear of

3. In the Christian context, Jesus said, "The Son of Man has come to seek and to save that which was lost" (Luke 19:10) and "the Son of Man did not come to be served, but to serve, and to give His life a ransom for many" (Matt 20:28b).

absurdity.)" (531). It seems that this entire novel—perhaps typically for postmodern novels—plays with the dialectic between meaning and absurdity. If it can find or create meaning, then at least the narrative world can be redeemed from meaninglessness. Yet in the end, even though Saleem appears to die (533), his death does not seem to redeem anyone or anything. The novel ends in ambiguity: ". . . it is the privilege and the curse of midnight's children to be both masters and victims of their times, to forsake privacy and be sucked into the annihilating whirlpool of the multitudes, and to be unable to live or die in peace" (533). There is no redemption here.

Saleem is not the only potential redeemer in the novel. For example, Saleem's Christian nursemaid, Mary Pereira, exchanges Saleem and Shiva at the hospital when they are born, saving Saleem from a life of poverty and violence (130). Later, at the end of the novel, Mary gives him a job at her pickle factory that leaves him leisure time to write his story. He refers to her as "the only mother I had left in the world" (526). But this hardly seems to be enough to qualify her as the novel's redeemer. Another possibility is Parvati-the-witch, the last of the Midnight's Children to stay faithful to Saleem. At the end of the 1971 Pakistani invasion of Bangladesh, Parvati-the-witch saves Saleem from becoming a prisoner of war by making him invisible and taking him back to India. This experience creates a sort of parallel to Christ's death and resurrection: Saleem says, "I learned what it was like, will be like, to be dead" (438), and then, "transformations spring upon him in the enclosed dark. . . . Did he not grow into the incarnation of the new myth of August 15th, the child of tick-tock—did he not emerge as the Mubarak, the Blessed Child?" (439). Eventually Saleem marries Parvati-the-witch, but she is then killed in Shiva's purge of the Midnight's Children. She does thus serve as a redeemer to Saleem, but because he is finally a failed redeemer, her own sacrifice seems to have become meaningless. One could also argue that Saleem's narrated audience, the pickle-factory-worker Padma, helps him to redeem the meaning of his life, or that the snake charmer Picture

Singh ("The Most Charming Man In The World") tries and fails—like Saleem—to redeem India.

Probably the best candidate besides Saleem to be the novel's redeemer is Saleem's son Aadam. Aadam is actually the child of Shiva and Parvati-the-witch, but because Shiva is the biological son of Saleem's parents and because Saleem marries Parvati-the-witch, Aadam becomes the son of Saleem. Contrasting Aadam with his own generation, Saleem says, "We, the children of Independence, rushed wildly and too fast into our future; he, Emergency-born, will be is [*sic*] already more cautious, biding his time; but when he acts, he will be impossible to resist" (489). Later, Saleem speculates that Aadam will not be a passive protagonist like himself: "I understood once again that Aadam was a member of a second generation of magical children who would grow up far tougher than the first, not looking for their fate in prophecy or the stars, but forging it in the implacable furnaces of their wills" (515). Ironically then, the novel ends with hope for a coming redeemer, but he is a redeemer unlike Jesus Christ—without "prophecy or the stars"—an existentialist redeemer who will create meaning through his own willed action: "in the implacable furnace" of his will.

## THE KITE RUNNER

Unlike *One Hundred Years of Solitude* or *Midnight's Children*, Khaled Hosseini's 2003 Afghan-American novel *The Kite Runner* does not display postmodern absurdism or skepticism about narrative form or the autonomous subject. Furthermore, it has little to say about postcolonial issues of cultural and racial hegemony and marginalization. However, it is of interest here for three reasons. First, it was a best seller in the first decade of the twenty-first century. Second, it comes from a primarily non-Christian culture, so Christian assumptions about redemption probably did not influence the author. And finally, it has been seen by a number of reviewers as a book about redemption. In the reviews printed in the 2005 Riverhead trade paperback edition, *The Buffalo News'* review says that "the culmination of the novel, too brutal and beautiful to reveal, demonstrates the author's capacity to bring life full circle in a great arc of grace and *redeeming* activity." The *Houston Chronicle* says, "In *The Kite Runner* Hosseini has created a wise, thoughtful book in which *redemption* and happiness are not necessarily the same thing." The *Kirkus Reviews* describes it as a "passionate story of betrayal and *redemption*." And author Isabelle Allende is quoted on the front cover: "All the great themes of literature and life are the fabric of this extraordinary novel: love, honor, guilt, fear, *redemption*."[4]

The novel clearly does set up an expectation of redemption. In the second paragraph of the book, the narrator refers to his "past of unatoned sins" (1). And in the next paragraph, a friend says, "*There is a way to be good again*" (2; see also 192, 226, 310). Thus, the entire book will present the possibilities for the protagonist/narrator, Amir, to atone for his "sins" and "be good again." One of his perceived sins is that his birth had caused the death of his mother, leaving Amir's father distant and judgmental. In the first portion of the novel, covering Amir's childhood in Kabul, Afghanistan, Amir hopes to atone for this sin and win his father's approval by winning a kite-fighting contest. Amir says, "All I smelled was victory. Salvation. Redemption" (65). He does win, but when his servant/ friend Hassan retrieves the prize kite for him, Hassan is trapped by three older boys and raped while a cowering Amir watches in secret. Much of the remainder of the novel is Amir's quest for redemption from his guilt over abandoning his friend Hassan.

At first Hassan himself is portrayed as the potential redeemer. He is innocent: "incapable of hurting anyone" (10). When he goes to retrieve the kite, he shouts to Amir, "For you a thousand times over!" (67). And when he is raped after finding the kite, he is described as having "the look of the lamb" that Amir had seen sacrificed in a Moslim ritual "to celebrate how the prophet Ibrahim almost sacrificed his own son for God" (76). Thus, Hassan could

---

4. Hosseini, *The Kite Runner*, preliminary pages; emphasis mine.

become the innocent redeemer for Amir. Amir even says, "Maybe Hassan was the price I had to pay, the lamb I had to slay" to redeem the relationship with his father (77). Hosseini could have shown Hassan suffering in Amir's place. Assef, the sociopathic young man who rapes Hassan, also vows to harm Amir, and when he challenges Hassan's loyalty to Amir, he says, "before you sacrifice yourself for him, think about this: Would he do the same for you?" (72). Yet Hassan's "sacrifice" does not redeem Amir. Despite Hassan's repeated attempts to regain his relationship with Amir, Amir rebuffs him, avoids him, and finally betrays him by framing him for a theft that he did not commit. When Hassan refuses to reveal Amir's betrayal, Amir says, "He knew I had betrayed him and yet he was rescuing me once again" (105). In the end, all of Hassan's redemptive acts merely leave Amir feeling shame and guilt. Hassan himself seems to recover from the effects of his rape, moves on, marries, has a son, and eventually dies during ethnic cleansing against his people, the Hazaras: a despised minority in Afghanistan. His suffering and death appear meaningless and of no value in redeeming Amir.

Hassan is survived by a young son, Sohrab, who offers another possibility of redemption. When Amir's friend had told him that there was "a way to be good again," that way was by rescuing Sohrab from a squalid orphanage and from abuse by the sociopathic Assef in Taliban-controlled Afghanistan. The story thus suggests that Amir can redeem himself by saving the son of the one who had tried to save him. Amir refers to it as "one last chance at redemption" (231). Amir is now the redeemer: he is redeeming Sohrab in order to make himself good so that he can redeem himself from the guilt and shame of his own past. This is indeed a kind of redemption, but it does not show an innocent redeemer suffering to save others. At the climax of the novel, Amir faces the murderous Assef to claim Sohrab's freedom. Amir has now attained a sort of goodness through his quest to find Sohrab, and he does suffer terribly as Assef beats him mercilessly. This beating is, in some ways, a redemptive act. In the midst of it, Amir says, "for the first time, . . . I felt at peace. . . . My body was broken—just how badly I wouldn't find out until later—but I felt *healed*" (289). Ironically, Sohrab must shoot Assef with his slingshot to save both Amir and himself from Assef. Even more ironically, when Sohrab later suspects that Amir is betraying him, he attempts suicide, and for the remainder of the novel, he remains aloof and mostly silent.

And so, in the end, *The Kite Runner* resembles *One Hundred Years of Solitude* and *Midnight's Children* in offering a failed or, at best, ambiguous redemption. Near the conclusion, Amir says, "If someone were to ask me today whether the story of Hassan, Sohrab, and me ends with happiness, I wouldn't know what to say. Does anybody's?" (357). This is not a traditional story of a heroic savior. In a thoroughly redemptive story, undeserved suffering or death brings about goodness. Sydney Carton's death in *A Tale of Two Cities* or Frodo's agony in *The Lord of the Rings* makes life better for those who remain. Amir's suffering only helps Amir. Perhaps this difference comes from a Moslem worldview. Certainly, this difference reflects a non-Christian view of redemption. When Amir learns that his revered father had committed sins which had contributed to Amir's own failures and suffering, a friend comments: "And this is what I want you to understand, that good, *real* good, was born out of your father's remorse. Sometimes, I think everything he did, feeding the poor on the streets, building the orphanage, giving money to friends in need, it was all his way of redeeming himself. And that, I believe, is what true redemption is, Amir jan, when guilt leads to good" (302). Instead of the innocent redeemer suffering for another to bring goodness, this pattern shows simple effort transforming guilt into goodness. Whether this pattern comes from Hosseini's Islamic background or from a postmodern culture, it definitely emphasizes a kind of redemption but creates a different kind of story from those built on an innocent sacrifice.

## THINGS FALL APART

Probably the most influential postcolonial novel of the twentieth century is Chinua Achebe's *Things Fall Apart*. Like *One Hundred Years of Solitude*, *Midnight's Children*, and *The Kite Runner*, this book deliberately overturns possibilities of redemption. Part One creates a lost world: the society of Umuofia, in the Ibo region of what is now Nigeria, around the end of the nineteenth century. The protagonist, Okonkwo, builds his family and his power by personal force and hard work. Various chapters present vignettes of life in Umuofia: farming, a wrestling match, bargaining for a bride, illness, a wedding feast. While the narrative makes Okonkwo and his family and friends increasingly real, two events disturb this world: the sacrifice of Ikemefuna and Okonkwo's accidental killing of a clansman.

Ikemefuna is a young boy given to Okonkwo's clan to pay the blood price for a murdered woman from the clan. He lives with Okonkwo's family for three years until the elders decide that the gods, through "The Oracle of the Hills and the Caves," have decreed that he must die.[5] This provides an almost pure opportunity for redemption: the innocent victim Ikemefuna giving his life to redeem his own clan, which is guilty of murder, and prevent a war. However, although his death does prevent war between the clans, his redemptive act ultimately fails. In the structure of the novel, it is presented as the first blow against Okonkwo's world. Before the killing of Ikemefuna, one of the clan elders comes to Okonkwo and says, "That boy calls you father. Do not bear a hand in his death" (57). Yet when he is killed, Okonkwo strikes the fatal blow with his machete because "he was afraid of being thought weak" (61). Consequently, Okonkwo experiences traumatic depression, and, more profoundly, his oldest son, Nwoye, begins to break away from him. Nwoye had loved Ikemefuna as a brother, so when Ikemefuna was killed, "something seemed to give way in-

---

5. Achebe, *Things Fall Apart*, 57.

side him" (61). Eventually this leads Nwoye away from Okonkwo, the clan, and the traditional ways.

Later, at the end of Part One, one of the oldest men of Umuofia (the same one who had warned Okonkwo not to kill Ikemefuna) dies. In the wild grief of the funeral, Okonkwo's old gun explodes and accidentally kills a young clansman. As a result, Okonkwo and his family must flee and spend seven years in exile in his mother's home village. Part One of the novel concludes, "if the clan did not exact punishment for an offense against the great goddess [Ani, the Earth], her wrath was loosed on all the land and not just on the offender. As the elders said, if one finger brought oil it soiled the others" (125). Such punishment of the whole clan for imputed guilt is the opposite of salvific redemption. In the Bible, Romans 5:12 says that " as through one man [Adam] sin entered the world, and death through sin, and thus death spread to all men, because all sinned." This universal imputation of sin is exactly what Achebe portrays on a more limited level in Umuofia. However, *Things Fall Apart* does not portray any redemption parallel to the biblical example: "For as by one man's disobedience many were made sinners, so also by one Man's [Christ's] obedience many will be made righteous" (Rom 5:19). Instead, Okonkwo must pay the penalty for his own (inadvertent) sin. Because of both Ikemefuna's death and Okonkwo's exile, Okonkwo's world begins to "fall apart."

In Part Two, larger events begin to destroy both Okonkwo's life and Umuofia itself. White missionaries come to the region bringing a "strange faith" (143). From a Christian perspective, it would seem ironic that Christianity would bring destruction rather than redemption. But of course, from both a postcolonial perspective and from the literary perspective of the novel, Christianity can be seen as simply another cultural force that may act in any number of ways, including breaking down the cultural world created in the novel. Achebe, however, does not resort to a simplistic analysis of the "strange faith." The missionaries and the accompanying white government officials do eventually destroy much of what Okonkwo loves and hopes for. Yet, at the same time, Christianity provides comfort to Okonkwo's son Nwoye: it "seemed to answer a vague and persistent question that haunted his young soul—the question of the twins crying in the bush [dying because the clan believed that they were cursed] and the question of Ikemefuna who was killed" (147). At the end of Part Two, one of Okonkwo's kinsmen says, "An abominable religion has settled among you. A man can now leave his father and his brothers. He can curse the gods of his fathers and his ancestors, like a hunter's dog that suddenly goes mad and turns on his master. I fear for you; I fear for the clan" (167). From Nwoye's perspective, Christianity brings comfort; from Okonkwo's perspective, it brings destruction.

Part One of the novel mainly creates Okonkwo and his world. Part Two shows Okonkwo and his world falling apart, in need of redemption. Part Three presents several different potential forms of redemption. One is the Christian religion, which does provide comfort and new status to various outcasts from the society of Umuofia, including Nwoye. However, these characters are not given prominence in the novel, and there is increasing conflict between Umuofia and the Christians, especially after the syncretistic missionary Mr. Brown is replaced by the exclusivist missionary Mr. Smith. In the end, this conflict is presented as destructive rather than redemptive. Another form of redemption can be seen coming from this conflict, when the people of Umuofia destroy the Christians' church (191). For Okonkwo, the destruction of the building functions almost like a redeeming sacrifice: "For the first time in many years Okonkwo had a feeling that was akin to happiness. The times which had altered so unaccountably during his exile seemed to be coming round again. The clan which had turned false on him appeared to be making amends" (192). Of course, a building is unlikely to carry the redemptive power of a true redeemer, and the sacrifice of the building does not provide any lasting salvation for Okonkwo or Umuofia.

The final and most significant potential redeemer in the novel is Okonkwo himself. By the end, he sees himself if not as the redeemer of Umuofia, at least as its avenger: "If Umuofia decided on war, all would be well. But if they chose to be cowards he would go out and avenge himself" (199). Vengeance is not the same as redemption because it is a violent act, bringing more guilt. But it is an act that restores in some sense what has been lost. And Achebe may well have a parallel with Christ in mind when he describes Okonkwo after his imprisonment by the white government: "they noticed the long stripes on Okonkwo's back where the warder's whip had cut into his flesh" (199). From Isaiah's prophecy (Isa 53:5), to the gospels (Matt 27:26, Mark 15:15, John 19:1), and through the epistles (1 Pet 2:24), the Bible emphasizes Christ's whipping. This alone is not enough to make a parallel, but the novel concludes with Okonkwo, like Jesus, hung on a tree. (In Acts 5:30, Peter says, "The God of our fathers raised up Jesus whom you murdered by hanging on a tree.") Taken together, these details suggest, if not a Christ figure, at least one who suffers to try to restore his lost world.

Ultimately, however, there is no redemption. The whites establish control—"*The Pacification of the Primitive Tribes of the Lower Niger*"—and the old ways of Umuofia will be lost (209). Okonkwo's body is taken down from the tree, but there is no resurrection. The white Commissioner decides to dedicate "perhaps not a whole chapter but a reasonable paragraph" to "the story of this man who had killed a messenger and hanged himself" (209, 208). One could argue that the writing of the novel itself (not just a reasonable paragraph but a whole book) is a redemptive act, preserving what can be saved of Okonkwo's world. But within the story, there is no salvation. To quote the epigram from Yeats' "The Second Coming":

> Things fall apart; the center cannot hold;
> Mere anarchy is loosed upon the world.

As in *One Hundred Years of Solitude*, *Midnight's Children*, and *The Kite Runner*, the novel ends in frustration or meaninglessness. Once again, redemption is an empty and impossible illusion.

⤳

Each of these postcolonial novels seems to play deliberately with the pattern of redemption, setting forth potential redeemers only to reveal their failures. The effects of such novels on readers seem to be very different from the effects of redemptive novels like *A Tale of Two Cities*, *The Lord of the Rings*, or *Le Petit Prince*. The popularity of this new kind of novel may indicate a cultural shift of tremendous significance, perhaps indicating that many readers no longer expect or hope for any final redemption in their lives. Of course, the move of Western society away from religion, and from Christianity in particular, is obvious and fits well with this literary trend. But it will be interesting to observe whether people can in the long-term abandon their desires for redemption when "resolutely" facing "nullity" (to return to Heidegger's terms), and, if so, how that will be reflected in the long-term popularity of works of literature.

# 6

## Poetic and Linguistic Redemption

MOVING NOW from narrative forms to poetic forms, this theory of redemption criticism enters more hypothetical territory. As mentioned in chapter 1, any story with a plot will unavoidably include some sort of fall with at least a possibility of redemption. Lyric poetry, however, does not require an obvious scheme of fall and rescue. A short lyric, in particular, such as a haiku, may do little more than describe a momentary scene. As such, it could be evaluated for its creativity (How effectively does it use language to create a world?), but this criterion alone is not enough to fit the pattern of redemption that I am claiming is essential to literature. However, there may be an even more elemental way that lyric poems employ redemption.

Consider William Carlos Williams's well-known piece "The Red Wheelbarrow":

> so much depends
> upon
>
> a red wheel
> barrow
>
> glazed with rain
> water
>
> beside the white
> chickens.[1]

1. Williams, *The Collected Earlier Poems*, 227.

It would be straining a point to see a narrative plot in this piece. Arguing that the "white chickens" need to be saved and that the heroic "red wheelbarrow" will do so would push the limits of even the most extreme forms of reader-response criticism. Of course, there is the possibility that this is pure mimesis: the reflection of a moment in the world out there. Williams considered himself to be an imagist, one whose goal is to create an image. Readers might simply appreciate the linguistic economy with which the poet creates this image.

However, I will suggest that such works employ a kind of semantic redemption in which it is not a character needing salvation but the very possibility of meaning that must be redeemed. As a teacher of literature, I have encountered many students who find this particular poem extremely frustrating. They complain that it doesn't mean anything—and they hate it. Only when they discover or are taught some key for making sense of it do they begin to accept and even enjoy it as a poem. Some "redeem" the meaning by contriving a fable about a farmyard where these chickens cannot survive without something provided by the wheelbarrow. Others impose a socioeconomic reading of how this wheelbarrow and these chickens are part of the chain of supply and demand that maintains the life of a nation. Some discover the notion that an "imagist" like Williams might be satisfied with the way meanings reside in objects such as those described here. In any case, the poem becomes "good" only when the reader rescues it from loss of meaning.

As another example of such purely semantic "redemption," consider the first stanza of Lewis Carroll's "Jabberwocky":

> 'Twas brillig, and the slithy toves
> Did gyre and gimble in the wabe:
> All mimsy were the borogoves
> And the mome raths outgrabe.[2]

Although these lines create the setting for a story, much of the content of this setting is empty upon a first reading because of the

2. Carroll, *The Complete Works*, 153–55.

nonsense words that Carroll has coined. As a result, readers must now "redeem" the meanings of these nonsense words. For example, if a reader does not imagine a meaning for "brillig," the poem will begin without its intended atmosphere. The reader must picture the "slithy toves" gyring and gimbling in the "wabe." Perhaps this goes back to simple creation. It is true that there is no apparent sacrifice to "redeem" these meanings. But the fact remains that there is in this poem, as in most, a considerable danger of failure that must be overcome by the poet and/or the reader for the poem to succeed.

I am suggesting now that the "fall" implied in such a piece is the possibility of a failure of communication. The act of redemption is the reader's own discovery (or imposition) of meaning. If this redemptive act fails, the poem fails. Obviously, such a "redemption" does not involve the sacrifice of an innocent victim (although I suspect that some of my freshman students see themselves as innocent victims of the required study of literature). So I cannot claim that literature of this sort fully conforms to a Christian pattern of redemption. Yet perhaps this helps to explain why few short lyrics attain the same level of greatness in the literary world as the greatest novels and plays.

Nevertheless, among the short lyric poems that are widely recognized as great literature, there is often an element of sacrificial redemption. Consider, for example, Donne's Holy Sonnet #14:

> Batter my heart, three-personed God; for, you
> As yet but knock, breathe, shine, and seek to mend;
> That I may rise, and stand, o'erthrow me, and bend
> Your force, to break, blow, burn, and make me new.
> I, like an usurped town, to another due,
> Labor to admit you, but oh, to no end,
> Reason your viceroy in me, me should defend,
> But is captived, and proves weak or untrue,
> Yet dearly I love you, and would be loved fain,
> But am betrothed unto your enemy,
> Divorce me, untie, or break that knot again,
> Take me to you, imprison me, for I

> Except you enthrall me, never shall be free,
> Nor ever chaste, except you ravish me.[3]

Throughout this poem, there is a repeated pattern of fall or loss followed by a plea for salvation. In the first quatrain, the pattern leads from "batter," "o'erthrow," "break," "blow," and "burn" to "make me new." In the second quatrain, the town is "usurped" (fallen), while the redeemer "Reason" fails to redeem. In the concluding sestet, the falsely betrothed (lost) lover begs the addressed savior ("three-personed God") to "divorce," "untie," "break," "imprison," "enthrall," and "ravish" in order to make him/her "free" and "chaste." It is true that the redeemer in the poem does not sacrifice for the narrator's salvation, but the basic pattern of loss and redemption is obvious.[4]

Naturally, such a pattern might appear in a poem about God by a Christian author. Consider a more secular example, such as William Shakespeare's Sonnet #116: "Let me not to the marriage of true minds":

> Let me not to the marriage of true minds
> Admit impediments; love is not love
> Which alters when it alteration finds,
> Or bends with the remover to remove:
> O, no, it is an ever-fixèd mark,
> That looks on tempests and is never shaken;
> It is the star to every wand'ring bark,
> Whose worth's unknown, although his height be taken.
> Love's not Time's fool, though rosy lips and cheeks
> Within his bending sickle's compass come;
> Love alters not with his brief hours and weeks,
> But bears it out even to the edge of doom.

---

3. Donne, *A Critical Edition*, 177–78.

4. Of course, readers who know the Christian background of John Donne and the theological significance of the "three-personed God" know that Jesus Christ is the implied redeemer in the poem. This, however, is a subtext and not part of the text of the poem.

> If this be error and upon me proved,
> I never writ, nor no man ever loved.[5]

This poem includes a number of falls: "impediments," "altera-tion," the "remover," "tempests," and such. Each is overcome by the steadfastness of love. In the third quatrain, "Time" is not merely time but is personified and carries a sickle, implying the figure of death, reinforced by "the edge of doom." Thus in this poem, love overcomes death. Although love does not die to bring redemption, love does "bear it out," suggesting a figure of strength, endurance, and possibly even suffering. There is nothing overtly Christian in the topic, yet it illustrates the idea that death—the ultimate fall—can be overcome. A quick scan of Shakespeare's sonnets shows that many of them deal with this redemptive theme of overcoming death: see, for example, numbers 1, 3, 12, 15, 18, 19, 55, 60, 65, 71, 73, 74, 106, 107, 126, and 146. Similar poems about redemption from death abound throughout the Renaissance.

For a more modern poem that employs a sort of redemption and has achieved great popularity, consider Robert Frost's "The Road Not Taken." The poem establishes a first-person narrator facing a choice:

> Two roads diverged in a yellow wood,
> And sorry I could not travel both
> And be one traveler, long I stood.[6]

Thus, the poem begins to create its own narrative, and in doing so, it uses the pattern of fall and redemption. The fall is the impos-sibility, implied in any act of choice, of experiencing two options simultaneously. The narrator is sorry that he cannot "travel both / And be one traveler" (ll. 2–3). The very fact that he chooses one path thus implies a kind of death: the nullity of the traveler who travels the other path. Here we return to Heidegger's notion (see chapter 1) of "Dasein" becoming authentic in facing resolutely the

5. Shakespeare, *The Complete Signet Classic Shakespeare*, 1750.
6. Frost, *The Poetry of*, 105.

possibility of "its own nullity."[7] Of the two potential travelers, one exists authentically because of the other's "nullity." The traveler of one path exists because of the figurative death of the self traveling the other path. The conclusion of the poem reinforces the notion that such a sacrifice is what creates meaning:

> Two roads diverged in a wood, and I—
> I took the one less traveled by,
> And that has made all the difference.[8]

I believe this poem has achieved literary greatness, or at least popularity, because of the force with which it shows that meaningful life is possible only when sacrifice overcomes death.

So far, all of the literary examples I have given have involved a narrative redemption (a sacrificial savior) or an act of semantic redemption. It is possible, however, that there may also be a syntactic act of redemption. Most poetry involves an element of structure that limits the poet's linguistic possibilities. Depending on the culture of origin or the form of a poem, it may require strictures of syllable count, rhythm, rhyme, parallelism, or various kinds of tropes. Each of these strictures implies a sort of syntactic danger: a possibility that the right word or phrase cannot be supplied to fulfill the expectations of the poetic structure. This idea that poets struggle with the "fallenness" of language is expressed in Lawrence Ferlinghetti's poem "Constantly Risking Absurdity":

7. Heidegger, *Being and Time*, 354.
8. Frost, *The Poetry of*, 105.

Constantly risking absurdity
and death
whenever he performs
above the heads
of his audience
the poet like an acrobat
climbs on rime
to a high wire of his own making
and balancing on eyebeams
above a sea of faces
paces his way
to the other side of the day
performing entrechats
and sleight-of-foot tricks
and other high theatrics
and all without mistaking
any thing
for what it may not be

For he's the super realist
Who must perforce perceive
taut truth
before the taking of each stance or step
in his supposed advance
toward that still higher perch
where Beauty stands and waits
with gravity
to start her death-defying leap
And he
a little charleychaplin man
who may or may not catch
her fair eternal form
spread-eagled in the empty air

of existence[9]

9. Ferlinghetti, *A Coney Island*, 30.

As Ferlinghetti says, the poet, "like an acrobat," is in danger of "absurdity"—failure of meaning—because he must "balance" his language on "a high wire of his own making": that is, the syntax of the poem. The difficulty of producing a word that fits the rhythm, rhyme, or other technical requirements of the poem while communicating an exact meaning implies a linguistic fallenness. The reader of a poem probably senses this fallenness subconsciously and therefore delights in the redeeming sense of the right word. We might then expect that the stricter the form (such as, say, the sonnet or the villanelle), the greater the poem that succeeds in overcoming its requirements to communicate.

This linguistic redemption may involve many factors. The sequential act of reading a poem forces the reader to expect certain linguistic pitfalls. For instance, once a rhyme scheme is established, the reader wonders (no doubt subconsciously) if each succeeding line will end with a word that fits the rhyme scheme without being trite or absurd. This problem is illustrated by Shakespeare's Benedick in *Much Ado about Nothing*: "I can find out no rhyme to 'lady' but 'baby,' an innocent rhyme; for 'scorn,' 'horn,' a hard rhyme; for 'school,' 'fool,' a babbling rhyme."[10] The same problem occurs with any linguistic pattern: rhythm, parallelism, simile, etc. Once an expectation is established, there is danger that the poet will not successfully meet that expectation to the audience's satisfaction.

Ultimately, this is an exigency of all language. Consider the nature of syntax. Although different languages employ different word orders, each language is a linguistic system that imposes expectation on the users of that system. Subjects need predicates. The expectation of grammatical completeness must be redeemed. As soon as a speaker says "the . . . ," a listener expects a noun phrase, such as "the cat." Such a noun phrase engenders a further expectation of a predicate: perhaps, "The cat sits." Obviously, this "linguistic redemption" does not include the death of an innocent savior. Yet even at this most elemental level of language, if there is a great

10. Shakespeare, *Much Ado about Nothing*, V. ii. 36–39.

loss or possibility of loss within the syntax followed by a great act of verbal "redemption" to complete or save the structure or meaning, that is what makes a great sentence. The memorable sentences are those in which we encounter a striking word or phrase where the possibility of banality is great. As Mark Twain said, "The difference between the almost right word & the right word is really a large matter—it's the difference between the lightning bug and the lightning."[11] Once Caesar says, "I came; I saw . . . ," he needs a redeeming conclusion. When Lincoln says, "government of the people, by the people, for the people shall not . . . ," only the most powerful phrase can save the hearers' expectations from anticlimax. And Roosevelt needs the perfect phrase to fulfill the linguistic expectations aroused by, "We have nothing to fear but . . ."

Probably the greatest example of the redemptive sentence is one that may well be the most widely known sentence in the world. Given the undisputed claim that the Bible is the best-selling book of all time, and given that many readers of that book consider John 3:16 to be the central statement in that book, one could find few sentences that are better known. The expectations established by the opening clauses of this sentence are overwhelming:

> For God so loved the world . . .

One wonders how the love of the almighty Creator for his creation could ever be measured or compared.

> that He gave His only begotten Son . . .

There cannot be a greater sacrifice than a parent's sacrifice of a child, and this is the eternal and ultimate parent making such sacrifice.

> that whoever believes in Him should not perish but . . .

What words could possibly express the result of such conditions without anticlimax?

11. Twain, "Lightning."

# 7

## Conclusion

I AM aware that, much like Ferlinghetti's poet, I am in this book "risking absurdity." I have made some quite audacious claims. Although I have called this a book of "Christian literary criticism," it is not that. I am proposing neither a way for Christians to read literature nor a way to read Christian literature nor a way to look for Christian doctrines in literature. Instead I am proposing a way of reading literature—based on what I believe is a universal principle that comes from Christianity—that explains the popularity and effectiveness of all literature for all readers. I am aware of the hubris of such a claim.

In 1628, William Harvey discovered the circulation of blood in the human body. (Actually, the discovery probably goes back to the Syrian Ibn Nafis in the thirteenth century, but the point is the same.) Was no one aware that blood flowed before this? Soldiers had seen blood spurt from wounds. Anyone who butchered an animal saw a heart, blood vessels, and plentiful blood. Yet before this, people apparently believed that blood was generated by the liver and slowly consumed by the body. So what was discovered in 1628? A better explanation of the structures by which blood circulates. There was nothing new in what blood did. But human minds had a new way of understanding what it did.

The so-called "modern" world spent half a millennium looking for structures to explain the surface of the earth, the movements of the stars, the behavior of matter and energy, the development of life, and the workings of the human mind. What philosophers call the *noumena*—the things themselves—were there all along. But the *phenomena*—the perceptions of these things—became codified in new ways. More recently, the so-called "postmodern" world has been pointing out that such codifications have problems. They may be discounted as relative, subjective, constructed. Yet the *noumena*—the things themselves—go right on "being," whether anyone codifies them or not, and most people are still happy to accept the modern codifications: that the earth is a sphere; that the planets revolve around the sun; that matter and energy are constant; that life seems to have evolved; and so on. What matters to most people is whether the code works. Does it get us from Europe to America? Does it get us from the earth to the moon? Does it get us to work on time?

Such questions become fuzzier when we deal with things less concrete, practical, and measurable. For instance, psychology has found bits and pieces of the "codes" that might explain human behavior, but in spite of claims by Freud, Skinner, and others, there is not yet a unified codification that fully explains why we act the way we do. And if we take a step further away from *noumena*—from things that exist out there in the world—to things that have little claim to exist out there, on their own, in the world, then the postmodern skepticism about codes becomes difficult to resist. How do we classify and explain ideas? beliefs? feelings? We can't honestly deny that such things exist. We can't say that they are not important in our lives. But we can't easily codify them either.

Literature is one of those things that has little independent, *noumenal*, existence. For more than three thousand years, written texts have been important to people. But literature, unlike a planet or a chemical element, is nothing but blots on paper until it takes on existence in a human mind. And because the mind of the author is not the same as that of a reader and minds vary from reader to reader, postmodernists can claim with some justification that codifying literature may be a vain project. For much of the last century, modernists attempted to codify it. The New Critical formalists tried to assert the independent, *noumenal*, nature of texts and to discover the structures that would unify each text, just as Newton's laws of physics had unified the universe. At midcentury, the structuralists went a step further, looking for underlying structures—literary periodic tables of elements—that would reveal the ways meaning is created in literature. But after the deconstructionists so gleefully pointed out that within any codified structure one could always find another contradictory structure, most postmodern readers abandoned the codification and looked for ways to link literature to things with more tangible kinds of being in the world. As a result, "theory" made literature into a vehicle for codifying other things: economic struggle, racial or gender issues, political conflicts.

For two thousand years, Christians have been claiming that God has given "the way, the truth, and the life." If that is true, then Christianity should provide the way for understanding all of life and, by extension, all things in life, including literature. In other words, Christianity should provide the "correct" way of explaining what makes literature work. Why do people value one story or poem and not another? What makes "good" literature? Marxist critics can claim that "good" literature illustrates social and economic justice. Feminist critics can claim that "good" literature reveals what healthy gender roles should be. But such views seem to relegate literature to the role of illustrating just one aspect of life. Christian criticism ought to be able to connect literature to the very essence of life. That is what I have brashly attempted to do here. I have little hope that many scholars outside Christian circles will pay any attention to the theory proposed here. But I do hope that anyone who reads this book will have a new tool (I would claim that it is the best tool) for understanding works of literature and explaining how they affect readers.

# Appendix

## *Survey of Christian Critics*

ALTHOUGH THE subtitle of this book is *Practical Christian Criticism*, I am not at all certain that it should be classified as Christian literary criticism. In a recent article in *Christianity and Literature*, Caleb D. Spencer delineates four kinds of Christian literary studies. The first is "scholarship in which the content of the inquiry is the distinguishing feature."[1] However, my book is not primarily about works of Christian literature like Milton's *Paradise Lost* or Jenkins and LaHaye's *Left Behind*, although such works do work well with my theory. The second kind is "that which sees literature as primarily a prompt for theological reflection."[2] My theory does come out of "theological reflection" and could be used to open theological reflections on literature, but my main goal is to apply the theory to literature for literary reflection—to show how literature works. Spencer's third kind of Christian literary study tries "to determine what Christianity holds to be true, beautiful or good; then determine what the work in question deems to be true, beautiful or good; then compare and contrast; and conclude by determining if the work is of value on the basis of the relationship between the two."[3] By contrast, my theory focuses on the structure of literature much more than on its views of truth, beauty, or

1. Spencer, "What Counts as Christian Criticism," 275.

2. Ibid.

3. Ibid., 276.

goodness, and I try to explain why works are effective rather than judging their value. The "fourth species of Christian scholarship . . . is practiced by scholars who claim that Christianity makes a *theoretical* difference to their reading because it shapes, forms, or constructs the texts that they engage," either through interpretive communities or through "unique epistemology or methodology."[4] One could perhaps claim that I am proposing a unique methodology, but it is a methodology that is not in any way dependent on the practitioner's belief system. Thus, my theory is not necessarily a Christian theory of criticism.

However, because I am relying heavily on Christian assumptions and doctrine in this book, I have classified it as a work of "Christian literary criticism." Therefore, to put my work into context, I need to look briefly at other works in this field. Christian criticism is certainly not new. The editors of *The Norton Anthology of Theory and Criticism* claim that around AD 400, Augustine of Hippo "fashioned a theory of signification that would dominate Western hermeneutics for ten centuries after his death."[5] And David Lyle Jeffrey says that "no work of literary theory for more than a millennium carried the weight and authority of Augustine's *On Christian Doctrine.*"[6] Augustine emphasized the ability of language to make allegorical significations, and he proposed "charity" as a key hermeneutical principle. Ironically, although these positions were formulated for the interpretation of the Bible, there is nothing essentially Christian about interpreting allegorically or reading to know and enjoy God and one's neighbor. Later, medieval readers who used Augustine's principles to impose Christian meanings even onto openly pagan texts (for example, finding prophecies of the birth of Christ in Vergil's *Eclogues*) may have been doing "Christian" criticism, but they were probably imposing

4. Ibid., 277, 278.
5. Leitch et al., *Norton Anthology*, 186.
6. Jeffrey, *People of the Book*, 89.

their own meanings more than they were interpreting the texts that they read.[7]

From Augustine through the nineteenth century, most Western literary criticism was done by readers who were at least nominally Christian, but, except for those who imposed Christian allegorical interpretations onto anything they read, their assumptions were not necessarily Christian. For example, Sir Philip Sydney's *An Apology for Poetry* owes more to the classical thinkers like Aristotle and Horace than to Christianity. Some evaluated the moral value of literature, but, again, moral values are not exclusively Christian.

Even into the twentieth century, when leading Christian authors and scholars like T. S. Eliot and C. S. Lewis turned to literary criticism, their approaches were not distinctively Christian. Eliot, in his 1932 essay "Religion and Literature," says that because literature can influence readers' behavior, readers should evaluate what they read using their moral and religious principles: "Our religion imposes our ethics, our judgement and criticism of ourselves, and our behavior toward our fellow men. The fiction that we read affects our behavior towards our fellow man, affects our patterns of ourselves."[8] This is a claim about the effects of literature on Christians, but it neither provides a definite way to interpret literature nor says anything distinctively Christian. And Lewis, in *An Experiment in Criticism*, looks at how different kinds of readers approach literature, but his "mature" readers are not in any way identified with any religious assumptions.[9]

Many literary critics who are Christian have simply examined and compared the relationships between their Christian beliefs and the worldviews of various works of literature. J. Hillis Miller claims that "even the best of the overtly Christian critics, Jacques Maritain, Allen Tate, or Thomas Gilby among the Catholics, Amos

7. Such readings might accord well with the principles of certain types of reader-response criticism.

8. Eliot, "Religion and Literature," 24.

9. Lewis, *An Experiment in Criticism*, 12–13.

Wilder, Nathan Scott, or W. H. Auden among the Protestants, though they may respect the individuality of non-Christian works, tend to make criticism a dialogue between their own religious views and the world views of the writers they discuss."[10] Such comparison of worldviews can be useful and interesting criticism, and it may be distinctively Christian, but it relies on the critic's particular theological beliefs and does not provide a well-defined critical methodology.

Another common way to approach Christian criticism is to ask, "What is the use of literature for Christians?" The stereotypical Puritan response to this question is that literature is either frivolous or false and therefore of no use—or even harmful—to Christians. However, a number of twentieth-century Christian critics have attempted to justify the use of literature by Christians. For instance, Sallie McFague TeSelle's 1966 monograph *Literature and the Christian Life* sensitively and carefully critiques previous attempts at Christian criticism and proposes that literature "can be of great importance to the Christian who is attempting to implement his discipleship by informing his trust in God and love of his fellows, so that his response to them will be profound and realistic."[11] Likewise Susan V. Gallagher and Roger Lundin argue that literature enables Christians "to respond to the order, beauty, and grace of God and his world and to the disorder that our sin has brought into that world."[12]

In the same vein, probably the best-known voice in late twentieth-century literary criticism for Christian readers is Leland Ryken, a professor of English at Wheaton College. One of his early books was the 1979 *Triumphs of the Imagination: Literature in Christian Perspective*, in which he essentially updates Sir Philip Sydney's 1580 *An Apology for Poetry*. Ryken defends the study of literature by Christians on the grounds that it can "teach and

---

10. J. Miller, "Literature and Religion," 33–34.

11. TeSelle, *Literature and the Christian Life*, 188.

12. Gallagher and Lundin, *Literature through the Eyes of Faith*, xxiv.

delight" (Sydney's echo of Horace's *dulce et utile*,[13]) and that both learning and pleasure are sanctioned by the Bible. The issues that he sees in other Christian critics as well as in his own work include "the nature of the religious viewpoint in works of literature, the extent to which the world view or moral perspective in a work of literature agrees or disagrees with a Christian world view, the nature of the Christian vision in literature, the values and dangers of literature in a Christian's life, and the theological ideas that explain and give sanction to the creation of imaginative literature."[14] This places heavy emphasis on the content of literature, and Ryken himself admits that "there are two levels at which Christian presuppositions add very little, if anything, to one's literary response. They are the level of artistic beauty and the level of mere presentation of human experience."[15] Thus, Ryken's criticism is useful when studying the ideas, themes, and worldviews of literature but gives little help in dealing with language and forms of literature. He also tends to deal with ideas that he labels as "inclusively" Christian: "ideas that *include* both Christianity and other religious or philosophic viewpoints."[16] Creation, for instance, and good versus evil are themes found not only in Christianity but in many other religions and philosophies as well. So, in spite of his evangelical and biblical emphases, Ryken's criticism is often more "religious" than "Christian."

My own theory draws upon Ryken in his use of a structuring archetype, called "the monomyth," derived from the works of Joseph Campbell, Northrop Frye, and others. Ryken says: "The monomyth is shaped like a circle and has four separate phases. As such, it corresponds to some familiar cycles of human experience. The cycle of the year, for example, consists of the sequence of summer-fall-winter-spring. A day moves through the cycle consisting

---

13. Ryken, *Triumphs of the Imagination*, 220–23.

14. Ibid., 121.

15. Ibid., 125.

16. Ibid., 124.

of sunrise-zenith-sunset-darkness. A person's life passes from birth to adulthood to decline and finally to death. The monomyth, too, is a cycle having four phases."[17] In Frye's *Anatomy of Criticism*, this pattern leads to the four genres of comedy, romance, tragedy, and antiromance. Ryken lists eleven plot motifs that are derived from it. I argue, on the other hand, that the pattern of creation, fall, and redemption is not merely a subsidiary pattern but is the ultimate underlying pattern from which the monomyth is derived. If Christ's redemptive act is the central fact of God's plan for the world, then the cycles of the day, the year, and human life are merely part of God's general revelation of his plan. Stories tend to follow the structure of the monomyth because the monomyth is derived from the foundational pattern of creation, fall, and redemption. Redemption is the essential element of the cycle of life and death. This should explain why the way a work of literature uses redemption determines how readers respond to that work, as I have tried to demonstrate in the previous chapters.

Ryken does occasionally emphasize the importance of redemption in literature. For example, in his 1991 book *Realms of Gold: The Classics in Christian Perspective*, he mentions in a chapter on *Macbeth* that "tragedy demonstrates a redemptive potential in suffering."[18] Later, he says that "to merit the title of Christian classic, a work must do more than portray a Christian viewpoint on a chosen aspect of experience. It must also give a convincing presentation of what is most important in Christian experience— the triumph of God's saving grace in the forgiveness of a sinner."[19] Therefore, at least when looking for a "Christian classic," Ryken does place salvation/redemption as the chief experience. He argues, for instance, that *The Scarlet Letter* is a Christian classic because the protagonist, whom he takes to be Arthur Dimmesdale, does experience salvation at the end. However, I disagree with

17. Ibid., 78.
18. Ryken, *Realms of Gold*, 67.
19. Ibid., 149.

Ryken here, since Dimmesdale is not saved by an innocent re-deemer but sees himself as saved by the redemptive power of his own suffering. Dimmesdale says, in his final speech: "God knows; and He is merciful! He hath proved his mercy, most of all, in my afflictions. By giving me this burning torture to bear upon my breast! By sending yonder dark and terrible old man, to keep the torture always at red-heat! By bringing me hither, to die this death of triumphant ignominy before the people! Had either of these agonies been wanting, I had been lost forever!"[20] Such experience may approach Christian salvation but it falls short of the pattern of Christian redemption because Dimmesdale pays for his own sins.

Ryken finally comes closest to the position I am proposing when he draws on the work of the twentieth-century Christian apologist Francis Schaeffer: "Christianity, claimed Francis Schaeffer, has a major theme and a minor theme. The minor theme is the fact of sin and fallenness. The major theme is salvation in Christ. Modern literature gives us truthful variations on the minor theme. Or consider the threefold Christian view of the person—good as created by God, fallen by virtue of its inclination toward evil, and capable of redemption."[21] This is a clear statement of the principles that my theory is founded on, although Ryken does not follow up on its general implications as I do.

Ralph C. Wood approaches my theory of interpretation when he says in *The Comedy of Redemption: Christian Faith and Comic Vision in Four American Novelists* that the "unexampled message of redemption in Christ finds a larger reflection and analogue in comic than in tragic art."[22] Wood analyzes works by Flannery O'Connor, Walker Percy, John Updike, and Peter DeVries to show how comic elements in literature reveal a Christian worldview more fully than tragic ones. Ultimately, however, Wood is making a claim about the nature of the Gospel more than about the litera-

20. Hawthorne, *The Scarlet Letter*, 215.

21. Ryken, *Realms of Gold*, 214–15.

22. Wood, *The Comedy of Redemption*, 23.

ture that may partially reveal it. He asserts that the Gospel is essentially comic rather than tragic. While this is an important claim, it does not provide a Christian theory for interpreting literature that is not comic, and Wood limits his critical theory by focusing only on literature written by avowed Christians.

In *People of the Book: Christian Identity and Literary Culture*, David Lyle Jeffrey argues that because of the centrality of a book—the Bible—to Christianity, Christians have always employed literary theories. He shows how both Jesus and Paul in the New Testament employed typological and allegorical methods for interpreting the Old Testament Scriptures. Furthermore, he argues that Augustine, as a trained rhetorician, consciously employed a theory of literary interpretation to both biblical and nonbiblical texts and that "no work of literary theory for more than a millennium carried the weight and authority of Augustine's *On Christian Doctrine*."[23] Jeffrey claims that, according to Augustine, "what prompts a *useful* reading is (consistently) 'charity, the motion of the soul toward the enjoyment of God for his own sake and the enjoyment of one's self and one's neighbor for the sake of God.' "[24] This implies that the intention of the author, as one's neighbor, is important for Augustine's method. Even more central is the notion that both biblical and nonbiblical texts can help to reveal the mind of God, the creator and the source of all truth.

Jeffrey rejects the postmodern critique that Christians are "logocentric," claiming that this critique arose from a somewhat arbitrary association of the "New Critics" and other formalists with Christianity. However, he redirects this critique to show that Christian literary theory should be logocentric in the sense that, because the Logos is the incarnate word of God, Christian readers use literature to search for the God who reveals himself through language.

23. Jeffrey, *People of the Book*, 89.
24. Ibid., 88.

One of the most elaborate recent forays into a Christian theory of criticism is that of Michael Edwards in his 1984 book *Towards a Christian Poetics*. Edwards begins with Pascal's themes of *grandeur* and *misère*: the greatness of the world deriving from God's creation and the wretchedness that has enveloped all things as a result of original sin. He argues that "the cosmology of Christianity is creation, fall and re-creation."[25] Literature, as an element of creation, must of necessity show "a ternary process, in which a positive is reversed by a negative, which is then reversed by a new positive far more powerful than the original."[26] Any narrative must follow at least part of this process, and Edwards shows fairly convincingly how tragedy and comedy build on the alternation of *grandeur* and *misère*. This "ternary process" matches closely with the creation-fall-redemption pattern that I have posited. In the end, however, Edwards's analysis seems too general. His theory is based on a biblical view of Christianity and does provide both a critique of other literary theories and a hermeneutic for interpretation of literature. But it really seems to be reducible to little more than the claim that literature is what he calls "dialectical." One does not need to be Christian to claim that there are opposites in literature. And Edwards's theory does not give enough emphasis to the crucial role of the act of redemption both in Christian theology and in the structure and experience of literature.

Paul S. Fiddes counters Edwards's theory by arguing that stories are not based on Edwards's pattern of fall and restoration but on the resolutions of anxiety over man's built-in freedom and limitation. In *Freedom and Limit: A Dialogue between Literature and Christian Doctrine*, Fiddes draws upon such theologians as Reinhold Niebuhr, Paul Tillich, and John Macquarrie to assert that the tension between freedom and limitation is more basic in the Bible and in literature than the U-shaped pattern of fall and

25. Edwards, *Towards a Christian Poetics*, 4.
26. Ibid.

rise. While Fiddes makes a convincing case for "the dialectic of freedom and limitation within human existence,"[27] like Edwards, he fails to account for the centrality of Christ's redemptive sacrifice in Christianity or for the importance of redemptive actions and language in literature.

Luke Ferretter's 2003 *Towards a Christian Literary Theory* takes up Edwards's critique of current literary theory and expands significantly upon the attempt to situate Christian theory in a postmodern context. Ferretter shows that deconstruction, Marxism, and psychoanalysis do not actually rule out the possibility of Christian criticism in spite of their expressed hostility toward Christianity. He then argues that the hermeneutics of Gadamer, Ricoeur, and Fish support, at least in principle, the kinds of interpretation that he proposes for Christians. He supports Edwards's position, claiming that "the most original and constructive work of Christian literary theory in the past 20 years has been Michael Edwards' *Towards a Christian Poetics.*"[28] Finally however, his own program, while supporting much of what Edwards says, remains at least as vague as Edwards's. He concludes: "It seems to me that this kind of criticism, which discusses the religious and theological significance of certain themes or motifs in a text, constitutes a way in which Christian literary and cultural criticism could and should, where appropriate, proceed."[29] But neither Edwards nor Ferretter proceeds much further with this kind of criticism.

In the end, I believe I can claim that, at least in emphasis, this book provides something that has not been done before. Working from Christian assumptions, I provide a methodology for analyzing literature and explaining what makes it effective. I do not limit my analyses to Christian literature, nor do I look for specifically Christian doctrines, practices, morals, symbols, or worldviews in literature, although those are useful things for Christian readers to

27. Fiddes, *Freedom and Limit*, 59.
28. Ferretter, *Towards a Christian Literary Theory*, 160.
29. Ibid., 178.

do. Even non-Christians who deny my premise that the pattern of creation, fall, and redemption is central to human life can employ my methodology, just as non-Marxists can employ Marxist methodology, nonfeminists can employ feminist methodology, etc. If they do so, I believe they will find that this method powerfully explains why certain works of literature become popular and/or endure as great works across long periods of time.

# Bibliography

Achebe, Chinua. *Things Fall Apart*. New York: Anchor Books, 1959.

Ash, Russell. *The Top Ten of Everything, 2007: The Ultimate Book of Lists*. London: DK Publishing, 2006. Online: http://www.ipl.org/div/farq/ bestsellerFARQ.html.

Camus, Albert. *L'étranger*. New York: Pantheon, 1942.

Carroll, Lewis. *The Complete Works of*. New York: Modern Library, 1936.

Christie, Agatha. *The Moustrap and Other Plays*. New York: Dodd, Mead & Co., 1978.

Derrida, Jacques. Excerpt from *Of Grammatology*. 1976. Translated by Gayatri Chakravorty Spivak. In *The Norton Anthology of Theory and Criticism*, edited by Vincent B. Leitch et al., 1822–30. New York: W. W. Norton, 2001.

Dickens, Charles. *A Tale of Two Cities*. 1859. Reprint, Garden City, NY: Nelson Doubleday, n.d.

Donne, John. *A Critical Edition of the Major Works*. Edited by John Carey. Oxford: Oxford University Press, 1990.

Dostoevsky, Fyodor. *The Brothers Karamazov*. Edited by Ralph E. Matlaw. Translated by Constance Garnett. 1880. Reprint, New York: W. W. Norton, 1976.

Eagleton, Terry. *Literary Theory: An Introduction*. Minneapolis: University of Minnesota Press, 1983.

Edwards, Michael. *Towards a Christian Poetics*. Grand Rapids: Eerdmans, 1984.

Eliot, T. S. "Religion and Literature." In *Religion and Modern Literature: Essays in Theory and Criticism*, edited by G. B. Tennyson and Edward E. Ericson Jr., 21–30. Grand Rapids: Eerdmans, 1975.

Ferlinghetti, Lawrence. *A Coney Island of the Mind*. New York: New Directions, 1958.

Ferretter, Luke. *Towards a Christian Literary Theory*. Houndmills: Palgrave Macmillan, 2003.

# Bibliography

Fiddes, Paul S. *Freedom and Limit: A Dialogue between Literature and Christian Doctrine*. Macon, GA: Mercer University Press, 1999.

Foucault, Michel. Excerpt from *Discipline and Punish: The Birth of the Prison*. 1975. Translated by Alan Sheridan. In *The Norton Anthology of Theory and Criticism*, edited by Vincent B. Leitch et al., 1636–47. New York: W. W. Norton, 2001.

Frost, Robert. *The Poetry of Robert Frost: The Collected Poems*. Edited by Edward Connery Latham. New York: Henry Holt and Co., 1969.

Gallagher, Susan V., and Roger Lundin. *Literature through the Eyes of Faith*. San Francisco: Harper & Row, 1989.

García Márquez, Gabriel. *One Hundred Years of Solitude*. Translated by Gregory Rabassa. First Perennial Classics ed. New York: Perennial Classics, 1998.

Hawthorne, Nathaniel. *The Scarlet Letter*. 1850. Reprint, Boston: Bedford/St. Martins, 2007.

Heidegger, Martin. *Being and Time*. Translated by John Macquarrie and Edward Robinson. New York: Harper and Row, 1962.

Homer. *The Iliad of Homer*. Translated by Richard Lattimore. Chicago: University of Chicago Press, 1951.

———. *The Odyssey of Homer*. Translated by Richard Lattimore. New York: Harper & Row, 1967.

Hosseini, Khaled. *The Kite Runner*. New York: Riverhead, 2003.

Jeffrey, David Lyle. *People of the Book: Christian Identity and Literary Culture*. Grand Rapids: Eerdmans, 1996.

Kalidasa. "Śakuntala and the Ring of Recollection." In *The Norton Anthology of World Masterpieces*, edited by Maynard Mack et al., 750–81. Expanded edition in one volume. New York: W.W. Norton, 1997.

Knoerle, Jeanne. *The Dream of the Red Chamber: A Critical Study*. Bloomington: Indiana University Press, 1972.

Leitch, Vincent B., et al. *The Norton Anthology of Theory and Criticism*. New York: Norton, 2001.

Lewis, C. S. *An Experiment in Criticism*. Cambridge: Cambridge University Press, 1961.

———. *Mere Christianity*. New York: Macmillan, 1943.

McMichael, George, et al., eds. *Anthology of American Literature*. 9th ed. Vol. 1. Upper Saddle River, NJ: Pearson Prentice Hall, 2007.

Miller, J. Hillis. "Literature and Religion." In *Religion and Modern Literature: Essays in Theory and Criticism*, edited by G. B. Tennyson and Edward E. Ericson Jr., 31–45. Grand Rapids: Eerdmans, 1975.

Miller, Walter. Introduction to *The Iliad of Homer*. Translated by William Benjamin Smith and Walter Miller. New York: Macmillan, 1945.

Mitchell, Margaret. *Gone with the Wind*. New York: Macmillan, 1936.

Morrison, Toni. *Beloved*. New York: Plume/Penguin, 1988.

Mott, Frank Luther. *Golden Multitudes: The Story of Best Sellers in the United States*. New York: Macmillan, 1947.

Poe, Edgar Allan. *The Collected Tales and Poems of*. London: Wordsworth Editions, 2004.

Richardson, Don. *Peace Child*. Ventura, CA: Regal Books, 1974.

Rignall, J. M. "Dickens and the Catastrophic Continuum of History in *A Tale of Two Cities*." In *Charles Dickens's* A Tale of Two Cities, edited by Harold Bloom, 13–25. Updated ed. New York: Infobase, 2007.

Robson, Lisa. "The 'Angels' in Dickens's House: Representation of Women in *A Tale of Two Cities*." In *Charles Dickens's* A Tale of Two Cities, edited by Harold Bloom, 27–47. Updated ed. New York: Infobase, 2007.

Robyns, Gwen. *The Mystery of Agatha Christie: An Intimate Biography of the First Lady of Crime*. New York: Penguin, 1978.

Rowling, J. K. *Harry Potter and the Deathly Hallows*. USA: Scholastic, 2007.

Rushdie, Salmon. *Midnight's Children*. 1981. Reprint, New York: Random House, 2006.

Ryken, Leland. *Realms of Gold: The Classics in Christian Perspective*. Wheaton, IL: Harold Shaw, 1991.

———. *Triumphs of the Imagination: Literature in Christian Perspective*. Downers Grove, IL: Intervarsity Press, 1979.

Saint-Exupéry, Antoine de. *Le Petit Prince*. Educational ed. 1943. Reprint, Cambridge, MA: Houghton Mifflin, 1946.

Scott, Sir Walter. *Ivanhoe*. 1820. Reprint, New York: Dodd, Mead & Company, 1941.

Shakespeare, William. *The Complete Signet Classic Shakespeare*. Edited by Sylvan Barnet. New York: Harcourt Brace Jovanovich, 1972.

Shelley, Mary W. *Frankenstein; or, The Modern Prometheus*. New York: Books, Inc., n.d.

Sophocles. *The Complete Greek Tragedies*. Edited by David Grene and Richard Lattimore. Vol 2. Chicago: University of Chicago Press, 1959.

Spencer, Caleb D. "What Counts as Christian Criticism?" *Christianity and Literature* 58.2 (2009): 273–81.

Stowe, Harriet Beecher. *The Oxford Harriet Beecher Stowe Reader*. Edited by Joan D. Hedrick. New York: Oxford University Press, 1999.

Susann, Jacqueline. *Valley of the Dolls*. New York: Random House, 1966.

TeSelle, Sallie McFague. *Literature and the Christian Life*. New Haven: Yale University Press, 1966.

Todorov, Tzvetan. "Structural Analysis of Narrative." Translated by Arnold Weinstein. In *The Norton Anthology of Theory and Criticism*, edited by Vincent B. Leitch et al., 2099–2106. New York: W. W. Norton, 2001.

# Bibliography

Tolkien, J. R. R. *The Lord of the Rings: The Fellowship of the Ring*. 2nd ed. Boston: Houghton Mifflin, 1965–66.

———. *The Lord of the Rings: The Two Towers*. 2nd ed. New York: Ballantine Books, 1965–66.

———. *The Lord of the Rings: The Return of the King*. 2nd ed. New York: Ballantine Books, 1965–66.

Tsao Hsueh-chin. *Dream of the Red Chamber*. Translated by Chi-Chen Wang. Garden City, NY: Doubleday Anchor, 1958.

Twain, Mark. "Lightning." Letter to George Bainton, 10/15/1888. No pages. Online: http://twainquotes.com/Lightning.html.

Wallace, Lew. *Ben-Hur: A Tale of the Christ*. New York: Harper and Brothers, 1880.

Williams, William Carlos. *The Collected Earlier Poems of*. Norfolk, CT: New Directions, 1951.

Wikipedia. "Harry Potter and the Deathly Hallows." No pages. Online: http://en.wikipedia.org/wiki/Harry_potter_and_the_deathly_hallows.

———. "List of Best-selling Books." No pages. Online: http://en.wikipedia.org/wiki/List_of_best-selling_books.

Wood, Ralph C. *The Comedy of Redemption: Christian Faith and Comic Vision in Four American Novelists*. Notre Dame, IN: University of Notre Dame Press, 1988.

## DATE DUE